"I'm pleased there are people like [Natalie] around the world. We can either ignore what happens in secular culture or we can engage in it, and in our own small way try and influence it for good. I know this book could help and inspire a generation of 'influencers' and help us all to take our place in God's great 'vision.'"

Martin Smith
Delirious?

"This book . . . was so practical and so refreshing that I read it right through. [Natalie's] message mirrors her lifestyle, and that speaks volumes to a jaded Christian 'rock star.' I needed to read this book just like any person out there looking for truth."

Kevin Max
dc Talk

"Natalie . . . is a dynamic woman of God. She is a Queen Esther who has chosen to put God's will first in her life. This book will challenge you to do the same."

Loren Cunningham
Founder, Youth With A Mission
President, University of the Nations

"We highly recommend this book to all youth who want to be 'Models for Christ' in whatever type of work they pursue."

Jeff & Laura Calenberg
Founders of Models for Christ, New York

"Her openness, zeal, and spiritual maturity ring a battle call for teenagers everywhere to *Ignite the Fire* in their own heart."

Chad Hovind
Pastor, Cumberland Community Church
Atlanta, Georgia

"This is a clarion call for young Christians to live lives that reflect Jesus."

Trent Sheppard
The Factory—Youth With a Mission
Harpenden, England

"Her story is fascinating, her passion infectious, and her challenge to the rising generation is compelling."

Lynne Rienstra
Transformation Teaching Ministry
Atlanta, Georgia

IGNITE THE FIRE

IGNITE THE FIRE

of Passionate Faith in an Awesome God

natalie moe

Ignite the Fire of Passionate Faith in an Awesome God

Second Edition

Published by Kregel Publications, a division of Kregel, Inc., P.O. Box 2607, Grand Rapids, MI 49501.

Cover design: John M. Lucas

Library of Congress Cataloging-in-Publication Data
Moe, Natalie.
Ignite the fire of passionate faith in an awesome God / by Natalie Moe.
p. cm.
1. Youth—Religious life. I. Title.
BV4531.3.M64 2003
248.8'3—dc22 2003015985

ISBN 0-8254-3342-8

Printed in the United States of America

03 04 05 06 07 / 5 4 3 2 1

To my wonderful family, who encourage my faith.

To the youth of this generation:
Have hope and passion;
be strong warriors;
rise up and
lead others in the right direction—
to Jesus Christ!

Contents

Introduction

So many teenagers lack hope. Being a fashion model has shown me how the world of pop culture contributes to that hopelessness. The prince of this world, the Devil, practices deception, distorting many young people's image of "beauty"—affecting their ideas about who they should be, how they should think, and what they should look like.

We all want to look our best, and we don't have to dress like John the Baptist in order to have a burning passion like he had; but an obsession with appearance can get in the way of John's message. He was the "voice of one crying in the wilderness, 'Make ready the way of the LORD'" (Matt. 3:3 NASB).

The wilderness of John's day was a lot like ours today. It results from clogging up our lives with the desire for material things, from feeling comfortable even though we're spiritually poor, from having little understanding of our need for God, from living rebelliously and selfishly—then wondering why life tastes like ashes.

Today, lurid pictures, dirty song lyrics, and movies depicting lust as love continually bombard us, twisting and scarring our minds. Too many of my generation are caught in this modern wilderness, wandering without purpose or direction.

Wherever I venture into this wilderness, I find young people who claim to be Christians but whose promiscuous behavior and foul language testify to another master. They acknowledge the *existence* of Christ, but He doesn't have any *relevance* in their daily lives. The Lord has led me to see His sorrow over this, as well as His longing to cleanse corruption and to set people free.

Yet most people don't want to hear the message!

If God could use *me* (a teenager when I wrote this book), He can do great things—beyond anything you can imagine—with your life too. The Lord wants to raise up a generation of young people who acknowledge His existence, who call out to Him not only when they're in trouble or praying for a future mate, but also for daily guidance. He desires a generation who know Him as Lord! The Lord longs to draw near to us, but we must first draw near to Him. He wants to raise up a generation of warriors who will represent Him in this wilderness and fight the good fight of faith.

Will you hear His call?

His promise to us is, "Those who hope in me will not be disappointed" (Isa. 49:23).

—Natalie A. Moe

Chapter 1

The Spark

The Journey from Modeling to Mission

The "spark" in my life was struck at the age of four. That's when I prayed with my mom and accepted Christ into my life.

I was born in Eugene, Oregon, in 1979. In my journey from being a model to realizing God's mission for me I've been down several roads. I want to first share with you how the Lord set my heart afire for Him along the way.

This first chapter of my story tells how I got from modeling to missions. The chapters that follow tell about some of my experiences and give some ideas about how you too can rise up, ignite the fire in your own heart, and then see God move!

I've been blessed with a Christian family who showed me from an early age that God exists, and taught me that Jesus loves me. They modeled values like honesty, respect for parents, and concern for others, always encouraging me to dream big and have faith.

Like many others, though, I took these blessings for granted, and the spark in my heart remained only a spark. I "believed" mostly because my parents were believers, and because believing was all I'd ever known.

When I was five years old, our family moved to New Zealand, where for two years my dad developed a salmon farm. I went to a country school and enjoyed life on a farm. Then we relocated to Sonora, California, which became our base for a couple of years. After that we moved to Chile, where my father set up another salmon farm. My mother homeschooled my brother, Steven, and me and incorporated Spanish into our lessons.

In Chile, I first recognized the condition of people in need. A little boy, Alejandro, was from a poor family, and he sold baskets in the center of town. He would linger, watching us play with the other neighborhood kids. Steven and I didn't know it was a social taboo to play with the poor kids, so we invited Alejandro to join us. At first, the other kids were hesitant to include him, but they soon got used to him. He turned out to be the best player at shooting marbles and was so proud when he won a bunch.

When we saw him the next day, he was very downcast. He told us that his father had been drunk and angry with him for playing instead of selling baskets. He said his father had taken his marbles from him and thrown them away. The spark in me flickered, and I felt hurt. I realized for the first time that life dealt some hard blows, although I didn't really understand why.

It made me sad and angry to see people in need when others had so much. Hungry people dug through garbage, looking for food that others threw away. One afternoon an old man knocked on our door. His suit was old and wrinkled, but he had a certain dignity. He humbly asked, "*Tienen pan?*" (Do you have bread?) We gave him some, and he asked God to bless us. It seemed so unjust for people to be hungry, especially when others wasted food. This experience simmered in my spirit.

In 1989, when I was about ten, my family moved permanently to Christchurch, New Zealand, and I enrolled in a Christian high school. There I fell into a complacent attitude: "Yeah, I believe but . . ." Bible class didn't penetrate my complacency, and although I went to church regularly, I wasn't drawn to the youth group activities. The spark started to smolder inside of me.

Sure, I claimed to be a Christian, but I hadn't taken time to develop a personal relationship with Jesus. I always stood up for Jesus, though I didn't really know why. In fact, I rarely opened the Bible. Like many others, I prayed when things got hard or when I was upset about something. I knew that God loved me, but I didn't search to find out *why*, and although I believed in God, I didn't try to love Him. I was a "babe in Christ" with a lot of growing to do.

At this point in my life, I was too busy looking for popularity and seeking the acceptance of my peers. I didn't like studying but loved to participate in sports—especially basketball, cross-country, and track (high jump). The competition gave me a certain amount of recognition and I loved the feeling of winning.

Modeling and the Genesis of a Dream

Even as a child, I thought it would be cool to be a model. This seems to be the "American Dream" for many girls. A career in modeling sounded glamorous and would bring me lots of recognition. In 1993, when I was fourteen, I started modeling after attending a teenage modeling workshop.

But believe me—I didn't feel secure about my looks. I never thought I was pretty, and my self-confidence was always on a roller coaster ride: my legs were too skinny, my face was too long. I couldn't forget the negative comments people made about my physical appearance. Of course, the compliments I received went right over my head! And although I was modeling and was gifted in some sports, I struggled with some of my school subjects, so my self-confidence was very vulnerable.

During this period, I learned how gossip could really hurt. Some students were spreading ugly rumors about a guy and me. The rumors weren't based on truth, but people love to believe the worst about somebody else.

I wondered how many other teens were going through similar experiences. How many other kids had problems with their self-image, how many had been hurt and were in need of comfort. That's when I discovered the spark in my heart was still alive. I began to dream of helping other teens deal with the hurts in their lives, to help them embrace and develop both their inner and outer beauty. This seed of an idea, though, had not yet found its time.

Rather, in my search to find meaning for my life, I tried having a relationship with a cool guy. I thought that if a guy (or lots of guys) liked me, that would fill the emptiness in my life. But the relationship didn't measure up because I was searching for a fire that only God could light.

By the end of high school, I was tired of the games everyone seemed to play and sick of the mask I wore. While I tried to appear secure, I felt only confusion about what I should do after graduation.

A Growing Time

When I was almost eighteen, an opportunity opened up out of nowhere. I was offered a job with the Navigators, a Christian organization that does discipleship on many college campuses and runs camps for young people in the summertime. I was to be a counselor at a summer camp in Colorado Springs, Colorado. I had no idea what to expect, and being the youngest counselor there made me feel a little inadequate.

While working with the kids, I met Barbara, the leader of the kids' camps. Barbara had terminal cancer, but she also had incredible energy and passion for life. She carried her medicine with her, and she wore a different colored hat each day to cover her head, which was bald as a result of the chemotherapy. A special light danced in her eyes, and everyone saw it the moment they met her. In spite of her grave illness, she was joyful.

I wanted to know her better, and to know that kind of joy too. Here I was—young and healthy, with my whole life ahead of me, yet totally confused and hopeless. This wonderful person, Barbara, fighting for her life, knew something—had something special—and I needed and wanted to have it too! I wondered, *Would she share her secret with me?*

One day, I felt especially afraid and confused about my future. As I walked past Barbara's office, I saw her and started crying. She saw me and invited me to come in. After she gave me a big hug and asked what was wrong, I told her about my doubts and fears. Then she asked me something that changed my life.

"Natalie, I know that you love Jesus, but have you ever made Him the Lord of your life?"

"I think so," I said. But as we talked, I realized that I'd never really asked Him to take control of my life—to teach me, to change me, to direct me, to speak to me—to have a relationship with me! I asked Him that day, and from the moment I gave myself completely to Jesus, my life has been an incredible adventure with Him at my side.

A Trying Time

After the summer job with the Navigators ended, I returned to New Zealand, still not sure which direction my future would take, but eager and ready to change the world. Little did I know that God had other plans. Instead of being a time of active work for God, it was a time of breaking, molding, and growing.

I developed a terrible acne problem. The spark inside of me had turned into a flame, and I wanted to tell others about God. But at eighteen years old, when acne should have been behind me, I felt so self-conscious about my complexion that I didn't want to leave the house. I tried everything to get rid of the acne and my self-consciousness about it. I fought it until I finally said, "Lord, teach me through this. What can I learn through this experience feeling so icky?"

Soon, God showed me the weeds I'd allowed to grow in my spirit. I saw that modeling had focused my time and energy on my outer appearance, and how much my happiness depended upon looking and feeling socially acceptable.

One day while shopping at the mall, I felt especially self-conscious (and extra icky). I'd reached the point where I didn't want anyone to look at me, and I was looking down at the floor. When I raised my head I found myself looking into the eyes of a young girl who had a large birthmark across her face. Our eyes met briefly, and we both quickly looked down. I recognized and understood her pain and embarrassment, and the Lord used that encounter to break my heart. In time my complexion cleared up, although every once in a while it would break out again and remind me about where my confidence was placed!

God was teaching me about the importance of outer beauty versus inner beauty. He was challenging me to focus more on my inner beauty, to be satisfied with who I was in the love of Christ. I began to venture out, helping others, in spite of my less-than-perfect appearance. Many of my friends were interested in what I had learned about inner beauty, and we had some good times together seeing how the Bible was relevant to their situations. I was able to encourage them to go on for God.

Moving Forward

During this time I had enrolled in Bauder Fashion College in Atlanta, Georgia. There I studied fashion merchandising as well as did some modeling. I set out, though, to enter the fashion world with a new mind-set regarding the meaning of *pretty*. Soon, just how much I had changed would become very apparent.

Before I could unpack my bags I was caught up in the swift current of a sprawling, bustling city that contrasted dramatically with my quiet farm life in New Zealand. My fellow students came from every strata of society. Several openly expressed their homosexual persuasion.

Living in a dorm-like apartment with six other girls, I quickly discovered that parties, drinking, drugs, and sleeping around were an accepted part of the social life. At this point I had to make a choice: Was I going to be like everyone else and fit in, or be different and live out my faith?

I chose to honor my faith. I would stand on the Bible verse that convinced me to be different, 1 Corinthians 6:19–20: "Do you not know that your body is a temple of the Holy Spirit, who is in you, whom you have received from God? You are not your own; you were bought at a price. Therefore honor God with your body."

If I were to get involved in drugs, sex, or drinking, that would mean I was sinning against my Jesus who lived within me. At that moment, I chose to stand for truth. I found it interesting that when I took a stand for Jesus, my faith grew and became even stronger in this challenging environment. I became even more assured that God's ways were the right ways.

People didn't understand why I chose not to disrespect my body, but they came to me for prayer when they were faced with problems or needed help in finding answers to difficult questions. From a young age I had been aware that people were in need, but at this point I became aware that I cared about those needs and people's feelings.

Still, it was a pretty lonely time for me, so I spent a lot of time at Barnes & Noble, drinking coffee and writing in my journal. About that time I participated in a program to help feed the homeless. A deep humility and true compassion were awakened in me when I saw how bruised the human spirit becomes from the hard knocks of life.

One morning soon after being with the homeless, I walked through the halls of the fashion college, greeting my classmates (all of whom were beautiful girls). For the first time I saw something that jolted me. Remember the mask I had grown tired of wearing in high school? Well I realized that here in this world of fashion and beauty people also wore masks—big time. But behind the masks these girls wore the same painful look in their eyes that I'd seen in the eyes of the homeless.

It was almost a shock to recognize this connecting link between people from two such different worlds. The shared pain I saw between the models and the homeless people made me realize that, regardless of the circumstances in one's life, rich or poor, without Jesus there is an emptiness that cries out to be filled.

Unexpected Blessings

The Model of the Year contest was fast approaching. The best modeling agencies in Atlanta would select the winner and be scouting for new faces. My fashion college was sponsoring it and I was chosen to be in the contest.

During rehearsals, I saw how tense everyone was and how very much they wanted to win. The night before the competition, I prayed for God to shine through me. I cried, as insecurity crept into my thoughts, and I asked God to help me gracefully accept whatever He wanted for me. I thanked Him for giving me the opportunity to participate—and for being with me.

As the competition began, everyone's nerves were on edge, the adrenaline pumping. One of the girls, Stephanie, asked me to pray for her. Some of the other girls joined us and we held hands. I prayed for peace, I prayed that we wouldn't fall off the stage, and I prayed that God would reveal Himself to each one of these young women. As I prayed, I felt sad that, like me not so long ago, they looked to God only when they felt a big need.

Since I had left all expectation of winning or losing in God's hands, I was awed when I won the contest. Later, one of the judges told me that when I first came out he noticed something different about me shining through. His comment thrilled me because of my prayer the night before asking God to shine through me! I knew that even in that setting, the favor and blessing of God could be seen.

Winning the Model of the Year title was a wonderful experience. It opened up more opportunities for me in the modeling world and, more importantly, would open up more opportunities for me to minister.

Mission Building

I felt a deep desire to grow more in faith. If God wanted me to continue working and witnessing in the tumultuous world of fashion, I needed to have a better understanding of God and His eternal plans and purposes. When I shared this desire with my parents, they agreed and were very supportive.

In October 1998, I was accepted into a program with Youth With a Mission (YWAM). The program, Discipleship Training School (DTS), was to be held in Hawaii and would include Bible study, seminars, and an outreach program in another country. This experience would provide the opportunity I needed to become grounded in my faith.

I flew to Hawaii three weeks before the DTS program to work as a mission builder—a volunteer who works behind the scenes to keep the missions base up and running. I was assigned to work in the kitchen preparing meals and cleaning up—a little less glamorous than a photo shoot, but it really was my favorite part of the job. After meals, people dining in the campus cafeteria brought their trays of dirty dishes and slid them through a slot to the kitchen staff. The other kitchen workers and I had fun, laughing and carrying on lively conversations as the other students came by. Those three weeks were a valuable time of preparation. I spent time with God, and I learned how to serve others before I began the five months of intense DTS study.

The DTS classes were blessed by many excellent speakers, each presenting a banquet of spiritual food. The truth of *who* God is fanned my spark into a flame. The more I meditated on Him, the more my love for Him and my ability to trust Him grew. He became bigger in my life and my confidence became securely anchored in Him.

Furthermore, I experienced the power of prayer and of God's Word. Both would serve me well as I continued on my spiritual journey. I realized the importance of praying for others and developed a thirst to pray about everything. I became hungry, too, for God's Word, which suddenly made so much sense and had so many applications to everyday situations.

Through DTS, the good news of God's salvation became a burning message in my heart, and I wanted to share it with others. All of this grounding would later be tested during a short-term mission trip to Hong Kong and China.

Decisions

As my time with YWAM came to a close, I felt God leading me to return to the modeling world for a season, to minister by word and example to other models. A Scripture given to me by a friend in New Zealand confirmed this call: "You must speak my words to them, whether they listen or fail to listen, for they are rebellious" (Ezek. 2:7).

Many of my Christian friends were unable to understand my decision to return to the modeling world. But I felt that God wanted to shine His light in that environment. His love is for everyone, so how could the fashion world not be a mission field too? It's hard—but certainly not impossible—to be in the world but not of it!

Still, I needed to check my motives and reinforce my identity before returning to the field of fashion. I had to be secure about who I am in Christ, or I might get crushed. The fashion industry focuses on outward appearance, and people in the business don't hesitate to criticize if a model's appearance differs from their perception of the ideal. Also, models might be asked to do things that they're not comfortable doing. If I wasn't sure of who I am in Christ, I might be tempted to do it. If a model is confident in what he or she believes, however, that model can say no and still be successful.

When asked how she could be a Christian *and* a model, one Christian replied that she tried to be a "model Christian." I like that.

Good News

Once I made the decision to return to modeling, I was happy to learn about a New York organization called Models for Christ. They encourage models (and professionals related to the fashion world) to take a moral stand based on biblical principles. After some prayer time with my family, I decided to go to New York and work with Models for Christ. Doing so would give me an opportunity to reach out openly to models.

On my way to New York, I stopped in Atlanta, Georgia. As a former Model of the Year, I'd been asked to present the awards and speak at the competition. My presentation would include the things I'd been doing during the past year. The event was held at Phipps Plaza, a large, upscale mall in Atlanta. I shared my experience from YWAM and the insight I'd gained about the importance of developing inner beauty. I was so blessed to have this opportunity.

Learning to Be Flexible

My mother and I arrived in New York on a lovely spring day in April 1999. We met Jeff and Laura Calenberg, the founders of Models for Christ, both of whom were very encouraging. We encountered little enthusiasm, however, in the waiting rooms of the New York modeling agencies. One agency was interested in working with me, but living in New York proved to be very expensive, and housing was just one of the several problems we encountered.

It became obvious that God was not opening up a place for me there. I was learning that His ways are not my ways. I wrestled with my disappointment, not understanding what God was doing. I kept asking, "Why would God bring me here only to lead me somewhere else?" God kept saying, "Trust Me. Although it doesn't make sense to you, trust Me."

About this time, I began to reconsider a modeling opportunity that had opened up in Atlanta before I came to New York. An agency there had expressed an interest in working with me.

My mom and I took a train back to Atlanta. As the scenery slipped by, I experienced waves of doubt and I questioned my understanding of God's call. Then I remembered this verse: "For I know the plans I have for you," declares the LORD, "plans to prosper you and not to harm you, plans to give you hope and a future. Then you will call upon me and come and pray to me, and I will listen to you. You will seek me and find me when you seek me with all your heart" (Jer. 29:11–13).

This became *my* verse, and I would hold tightly to the words.

Mission

While we were in Atlanta, God placed a desire in my heart to start a chapter of Models for Christ there. I would step forward in faith, learning to trust Him more and more, especially when I couldn't see the way. Like it says in Hebrews 11:1, "Now faith is being sure of what we hope for and certain of what we do not see." I would move forward in faith.

The Atlanta agency offered a contract and I began working. But the road still had some unexpected twists ahead. I had arrived during a slow period, and there weren't many modeling jobs available. That's when I felt the urge to write this book. This was so unusual for me, because I'd never before had the desire to write. The off-season in the modeling industry also gave me time to pray for the Models for Christ vision to become a reality. I certainly had the time, and God seemed to be saying, "Move forward."

Now that you know a little about me, and as you hear the rest of my story, I'd like to share some other things that God has taught me, as well as things He has accomplished in my life. Because this book is about God and His Word, it includes a lot of Scripture. Please don't skip over it.

In case you don't know Jesus and His amazing love and forgiveness, check out chapter 12, "Steps to Salvation." It contains just what it says—simple steps that lead to salvation. Read it. It could change your life.

Chapter 2

God's Burning Love

Ask God to Show His Love to You

One thing that radically changed my walk with God was realizing how much He loved me. To explain this, I need to back up a little with my story—back to my Youth With a Mission training. During the first week of Discipleship Training School in Hawaii, I became very ill. The doctor initially diagnosed mono, and I was so sick that the doctor thought I might have to return home.

While everyone else was attending seminars and listening to speakers teach about God's love, I was lying flat on my back staring at the ceiling. I felt so helpless and frustrated. I was missing wonderful lessons—lessons I needed, particularly the ones about God's love. That was an area I had struggled with because I was so aware of my failures. My temper, my tongue, and my pride could trip me up so easily; I thought I had so many unlovable things about me that I wondered, *How could God love me?* As I lay there feeling bitter about my situation, the thought came to me, "Ask God to be your teacher." Soon, He began to reveal the depth and scope of His love.

Once while I was sleeping, I dreamed that Jesus and I were sitting on a bridge, dangling our feet in a river. The dream was so vivid I could almost feel the coolness of the water. When I awoke, I knew that Jesus was there in the room with me. He began right then to teach me and to reveal how much He loved me, even though all I could do was lay on my bed, unable to do anything for Him. But what I could do for Him at that moment wasn't important. He was teaching me to just *be*.

I didn't need to do things to impress God or earn His love; all I needed to do was accept His amazing love. No matter what our limitations, that's all we need to do—accept His love.

Romans 11:6 says, "And if by grace, then it is no longer by works; if it were, grace would no longer be grace." We don't have to work for God's love. He gives it to us out of grace—out of a generous heart.

It was such a comfort, such a relief just to let God love me. Shortly after this, I experienced God's healing touch. I recovered my strength and was able to continue with Discipleship Training School. Not only had my physical body been strengthened, but my spirit had been strengthened too. I was experiencing the comfort expressed in Psalm 34:18: "The LORD is close to the brokenhearted and saves those who are crushed in spirit."

Growing in Love

The Bible assures us over and over of God's love, but we often fail to comprehend it. The love of God is something that He wants you to know, believe, and meditate upon until it becomes as real to you as your eyebrows. One of my favorite Bible passages is, "Are not two sparrows sold for a penny? Yet not one of them will fall to the ground apart from the will of your Father. And even the very hairs of your head are all numbered. So don't be afraid; you are worth more than many sparrows" (Matt. 10:29–31). You are not just a face, lost in the crowd, or a mere statistic.

Over the past several years I've done a fair amount of plane travel. When I fly I look out the window and see miniature people, driving toy-sized cars along ribbons of highway. I think, *Can God really know each one of us, individually? Can He really see me?* Then I recall His assurance: "Fear not, for I have redeemed you; I have summoned you by name; you are mine" (Isa. 43:1b). God knows me by name. He knows *you* by name.

The Hugeness of God

The Bible reveals the greatness of the mighty God I serve. God's creation—the universe and the world around us—gives meaning to words like *glorious* and *powerful*. You can see His hand in the beauty and greatness of nature—a brilliant sunset, a fragile flower, a lone bird soaring in the sky; all have the Creator's signature. My trust is not only in a loving God, but in a very powerful God, who is worthy of worship. Before the greatness of our God, I have to kneel in humility, as worship takes on a new dimension, one in which words alone become inadequate.

When you realize who God is and allow yourself to be awed by His amazing hugeness, you'll become and remain passionately on fire for His Word. You'll understand the meaning of Proverbs 1:7: "The fear of the Lord is the beginning of knowledge."

I don't know what kind of experience or understanding you have of love, but God's love surpasses anything you'll ever know. His love doesn't waiver like human love sometimes does. The Bible tells us in Psalm 145:13b, "The Lord is faithful to all his promises." That means we can trust Him.

Receiving the Message

Once, during worship time at a Christian youth retreat in Florida, God revealed His love to me through a song. I understood that in a way, God was singing this song to me and to all the other teens there.

He longs to relate to us, but we frequently block His messages. During worship we think about what someone else is wearing, whether a certain guy or girl is cute, or if we look good standing in a particular pose. Worship is meant to be a time when we focus on God, not on others or ourselves.

Imagine being in a movie theater. The lights dim and everyone and everything disappears as we concentrate on the screen. That's the way worship should be. We should focus on God while everyone and everything else fades into the background.

While God is trying to get across to us how very much He loves us, the Devil is trying to undermine God's truth. Satan distracts our attention from the message, causing us to miss out on it and doubt God's love. It used to be that when the Devil whispered to me, "Who are you anyway?" I'd immediately be filled with doubts and my self-confidence would plummet. Who are we going to believe—the Devil's lies that cause us to feel bad, or a loving God who says, "Who shall separate us from the love of Christ?" (Rom. 8:35)? No one and nothing can separate us from God's perfect love unless we allow it!

God Is Love

This is a foundational truth upon which we can build our lives. Knowing how much God loves us gives us confidence. No matter what's happening around us or to us, knowing that God loves us gives us perspective. Our outlook becomes like climbing a mountain to get a better vantage point; everything below falls into place.

Confession and Forgiveness

Don't let anybody tell you that your sins are too awful, and that God won't forgive you. The Bible assures us, "If we confess our sins, he is faithful and just and will forgive us our sins and purify us from all unrighteousness" (1 John 1:9). When confession comes from a repentant heart, the Lord forgives our sin. To repent means you're sorry for the wrong (sin), you stop doing that wrong thing, and you strive to please God. (To learn what pleases God, we read and study our Bibles.) In fact, He promises, "Though your sins are like scarlet, they shall be as white as snow" (Isa. 1:18).

It's a good idea to keep our sin accounts short. We should quickly confess when we slip up and do or say things that are sinful. Otherwise, the guilt of our unconfessed sin separates us from God (as with Adam and Eve when they hid from God in the Garden of Eden). This separation opens a door for the Devil. He comes in and lies to us, saying, "How could God love a sinner like you?" Don't listen to the lies! Confess what you've done and ask God to help you not to do it again. Then move on!

While forgiveness is easy for us to obtain, it cost Jesus a great price. So we should never take sin or forgiveness lightly. Some people I knew in high school used to go to parties and do things they were ashamed of, but they planned to confess later. God, though, is not fooled.

Doing something bad has its consequences. A young girl, a friend of our family, was badly injured by a drunk driver. If you drink and drive and have an accident, you, your passengers, or the people in the other car may be injured or paralyzed. Of course God will forgive you. He knows our hearts and our motives, but you'll still have to live with consequences that could blow the rest of your life. As Paul wrote, "Shall we go on sinning so that grace may increase? By no means! We died to sin; how can we live in it any longer?" (Rom. 6:1–2).

God has a burning love for you. Let Him love you into a fresh new life, so that "you, being rooted and established in love, may have power, together with all the saints, to grasp how wide and long and high and deep is the love of Christ, and to know this love that surpasses knowledge—that you may be filled to the measure of all the fullness of God" (Eph. 3:17–19).

THIS WEEK, ASK GOD TO SHOW HIS LOVE FOR YOU.

For Discussion:

- Explain how it feels to be loved by someone.
- Have you accepted and embraced God's love?
- How can you share God's love this week with someone you know?

Meditate on the meaning of these verses:

> The LORD is gracious and compassionate, slow to anger and rich in love. . . . The LORD is righteous in all his ways and loving toward all he has made. (Ps. 145:8, 17)

Read the story of the prodigal son in Luke 15:11–32. The father in this example represents God. Have you let God welcome you home like that father welcomed his child?

To get a clearer understanding of just how well God knows you, read Psalm 139.

REFINING FIRE

Burning with Love is the fire of God,

Discipline that molds from above.

Melting, mending, changing me to gold,

I willingly submit instead of being told.

I am so wretched, such a prideful heart,

I would give anything for your peace
to never part.

So burn with your love

That never ceases from above.

Come down with your fire,

Mold, mend, and change my desire.

Blind Faith

Blurry, blinding, confusion
Waiting, waiting for you.

Your face I long to gaze upon,
I cry out from the depths of my soul,
Every part of my body longs for revelation
Why are you so quiet?

Yet so close.

Longing in my soul,
Yearning in my spirit
Pour over me like the crashing waves of the sea.
Comfort me, hold me,
Take care of me.
Hear me when I cry out,
Answer from your throne,
Why are you so quiet?

Yet so close.

Have mercy on your servant,
I will hope in you, I will never let go.

I will praise you because I trust you will be faithful.
Joy beyond containment,
Blurry, blinding confusion
Waiting, waiting for you
Even though you are quiet,

Yet so close.

Chapter 3

Fiery Faith

Step Out in Faith

Joy in living each moment for Him,
soaring through life like the eagle high in the air,
gliding in peace, knowing by faith
that the wind will hold him up
even though he can't see it.

—Natalie Moe

Faith is being sure of what we hope for and certain of what we do not see.

Hebrews 11:1

Many times I've cried out to God. I've asked Him to reveal my future or show me a little of what lies ahead. But if I know what's coming, why would I need faith? One of my favorite and most encouraging Bible verses is Isaiah 40:31: "But those who hope in the Lord will renew their strength. They will soar on wings like eagles; they will run and not grow weary, they will walk and not be faint."

Hold to Faith

I encourage you to read the book of Job. One day as I was sitting on my bed reading the Bible, I sensed God telling me to read the book of Job, a book in the Bible I had never read. I was quite disappointed as I read the first few chapters, but then realized that God wanted to speak to me through Job's life and what he learned.

Job was faithful to God. He was wealthy and had a big family, but the Devil said to God, "I'll bet Job, your faithful servant, would deny you and curse you if his riches and blessings were taken away from him."

God, though, had confidence in Job's faithfulness and allowed the Devil to test him. The Devil stripped Job of everything—his kids, his wealth, and his health. But Job didn't curse God. Instead he cried out to God, asking Him for help to understand why these bad things were happening. Job felt that if he understood *why* God had allowed such things, he could better accept them.

Finally, God spoke to Job, revealing something of His greatness. In a voice like thunder, God reminded Job that He commanded the morning, and enclosed the sea, and formed the earth (see Job, chapters 38 through 41). These beautiful chapters reveal some of God's hugeness. When Job's eyes were opened to who God was, he declared, "I know that you can do all things; no plan of yours can be thwarted. . . . My ears had heard of you but now my eyes have seen you" (Job 42:2, 5). Job remained faithful, and saw a glimpse of the greatness of God that put his own life into perspective. And God gave to him more than he had originally—more wealth, even more children.

Job's case is extreme, and it's unlikely we'll ever have to go through anything like he did. But the lesson that Job learned can be applied to our problems in today's world. Like Job, we too must put our hope and trust in God, because He is ultimately in control. He will eventually work out all of our situations for our good. When we believe and hold on to this truth, then like Job we too will have confidence in God's perfect plan, regardless of what is happening around us or to us.

Good Versus Evil

We are in a spiritual battle made up of two sides—good and evil. The Devil (Satan) doesn't want us to have faith in God. Faith is a powerful force that can shut down the Devil's plans to defeat you.

Past: Paradise Lost

Satan didn't just appear out of nowhere. The Bible says he was a top angel in heaven who one day decided he wanted to be like God. (You can read about it in Isaiah 14:12–15 and Revelation 12:7–12.) Although the Bible doesn't give a lot of detail, Satan rebelled against God and was kicked out of heaven. His next appearance was in the Garden of Eden.

When Adam and Eve fell for the Devil's lies, that sin affected all creation—including us. Only one thing could save us: Jesus came to earth and died for our sins. Jesus said, "[Satan] comes only to steal and kill and destroy" (John 10:10). Satan is at work in the world now, but we don't have to be fooled by him.

Whether you realize it or not, a battle is happening right now, on earth, in the invisible realm. Ephesians 6:12 says, "For our struggle is not against flesh and blood, but against the rulers, against the authorities, against the powers of this dark world and against the spiritual forces of evil in the heavenly realms." The Devil is trying to deceive you into thinking God doesn't exist and that sin is harmless.

It sounds like a scene from the movie *Lord of the Rings,* with the forces of evil fighting for control against the forces of good, doesn't it? But this battle is real. You may not fully understand the ongoing battle between good and evil. It may take a while for the reality of it to take hold in your mind. And that's okay. Ask God to help you understand. Read your Bible and talk to the youth pastor at your church. What's important for you to know right now is this: God is more powerful than Satan, and we as Christians are on the winning side!

You may wonder, *Why didn't God just stop the Devil long ago?* God is certainly more powerful and could do it. But if God stopped the Devil, getting rid of evil, He would have to get rid of us as well, since we do evil, too. Because He loves us so much, God has chosen a better way. He sent Jesus not only to endure evil and suffering on the cross as payment for our sins, but also to triumph over sin in His resurrection. God decided that it was better to bring good out of evil than to destroy His creation, which (again) would have included us. Instead, we can always look to the Cross and see the hope and victory it represents.

Present

As the battle between good and evil rages, we are to live and walk by faith. To be victorious, Ephesians 6:16 tells us, "Take up the shield of faith, with which you can extinguish all the flaming arrows of the evil one." This verse reminds me of TV's *Star Trek,* when the captain orders the shield to be put up to protect the Enterprise. (I'm not really a *Star Trek* fan but I remember that part!) Imagine yourself surrounded by a shield of faith in God—because you are!

Future: Paradise Regained

God sees the world and time differently than we do. He sees not only the past and present; He sees the future, too. Right now, in the present, God is saddened by the sin we commit and the pain we experience. But He can also see the evil in relation to the future (eternity), when sin will lose its power and God will transform us. We will share eternity with Him in a sinless world. That was God's best plan for us when He created Adam and Eve. Of course God hated the pain and suffering His Son endured on the cross (Sin can have a high price!), but He also saw that His death and resurrection would triumph over evil and provide salvation for us. Jesus has the victory—and through Him, we do too! Just remember, "The one who is in you [Jesus] is greater than the one who is in the world [Satan]" (1 John 4:4).

Spiritual Weapons

I used to get into some low times. I'd feel hopeless—almost desperate and useless. I'd feel like a big dark cloud had descended upon me. I'm thankful that my mom taught me to recognize that those negative feelings were the Enemy's work and were not from God. She encouraged me to fight back with the truth of God's Word. So one night when I was lying in bed, thoughts of hopelessness and doubt flooding my mind, I made a decision: I'd do what my mother said to do. I sat up in bed and said, "In the name of Jesus, go away Devil. Leave me alone. God loves me and promises me that He has good plans for me because I'm His child."

The instant I said this, the peace that Jesus promised, the peace that passes all understanding (Phil. 4:7), wrapped around me like a warm blanket. The name of Jesus is powerful! Now I know how to call upon the name of Jesus to get rid of these evil thoughts. Like it says in 1 Peter 5:8–9, "Be self-controlled and alert. Your enemy the devil prowls around like a roaring lion looking for someone to devour. Resist him, standing firm in the faith." Resist! We can have victory over evil.

Your Identity, God's Will

You'll discover two great blessings in your walk with God:

- Knowing *who you are in Christ*
- Knowing that you are walking in His will

When you live your life according to the expectations of others, you get pain, disappointment, and discouragement. When you follow God's plans for you, you walk in His approval. Don't succumb to the world's expectations! Strengthen your resolve and follow God's plan for you. "For you did not receive a spirit that makes you a slave again to fear, but you received the Spirit of sonship. And by him we cry, 'Abba, Father'" (Rom. 8:15). (*Abba* is an Aramaic word, similar to *Daddy* in English.)

When we fully accept the wonderful truth that God really loves us, we can know for certain that He has a purpose, a plan, and a mission for our lives: "We are God's workmanship, created in Christ Jesus to do good works, which God prepared in advance for us to do" (Eph. 2:10).

What are these good works we're supposed to do? Anything we do to help someone in the name of Jesus qualifies as a good work: offering encouragement to a friend in need, making dinner when Mom or Dad is tired, giving a hungry family a bag of groceries, comforting a dying person, or sharing the gospel of life with someone. Whether you're in school or at work, remember—your environment is your mission field.

Life in the Faith Zone

Just as God's truths are the opposite of the Devil's lies, doubt is the opposite of faith. Doubt is an arrow that the Devil uses on us, just like he did on Adam and Eve. To undermine our obedience to God, the Devil wants us to doubt God's love and truths. But God wants us to live in the faith zone. He wants to give us a good life, and reveal His truths to us.

But sometimes our doubting prevents Him from giving good things to us. When something big or scary comes my way, faith knocks at the door—but so does doubt. It's decision time: Will I answer the faith knock or the doubt knock? If I answer the doubt knock, my feelings will spiral downward and I'll be filled with doubt in myself. Then self-pity walks in and whines, "You're not good enough."

That leads to:

- Doubting God
- Doubting God's love for me
- Doubting the very existence of a loving and caring God

But what happens when I answer the faith knock?

- I claim the promises of God—promises that enable me to stand against the Enemy.
- God is able to move on my behalf because my hand is in His, and He knows I'll obey.

Instead of the downward spiral, I climb out of the pit. The

process starts with faith that I can "do all things through Christ who strengthens me" (Phil. 4:13 NKJV).

I trust that whatever happens, God has a plan and a purpose for me, and He will reveal His plan and help me achieve His purpose. I can trust His love for me and know that He will take care of me.

Tempted to Doubt

Doubt is a terrible place to be. I've wallowed in doubt for hours—even days. But faith and doubt are choices, and we are presented with those choices every day. I'm learning to recognize doubt and to choose the faith way. Sometimes I fail, but I quickly reaffirm that I am a child of God, a chosen daughter of the King.

Whenever I doubt my Father, it's because I've forgotten who I am in Christ and to Whom I belong. That's when I'm "like a man who looks at his face in a mirror and, after looking at himself, goes away and immediately forgets what he looks like" (James 1:23–24).

Throw down your pride, and say no to every lie the Devil throws at you. Take up your cross, even though you might be scared and can't see what lies ahead. Remember that our Father sees all, knows all, and will strengthen your faith, especially as you read the Bible: "Consequently, faith comes from hearing the message, and the message is heard through the word of Christ" (Rom. 10:17).

We can be thankful that God is patient, forgiving, and merciful. When we recognize our doubt and turn to Him, we can quickly embrace our faith again without losing ground. Pretty neat, huh?!

The Faith Gym

To grow strong, our muscles need resistance training—to push against a force, like weights. The same thing goes for our faith; faith sometimes needs to push against resistance, like temptation, to grow strong. But God knows just how much force you can take: "God is faithful; he will not let you be tempted beyond what you can bear. But when you are tempted, he will also provide a way out so that you can stand up under it" (1 Cor. 10:13). Isn't that a great promise? You don't have to give in to temptation. You can look for a way out.

So stand strong in times of testing. God doesn't want us to be afraid of trials and problems: "The testing of your faith develops perseverance. Perseverance must finish its work so that you may be mature and complete, not lacking anything" (James 1:3–4). When you live in the faith zone, the Christian life can be a challenge. It's definitely *not* boring.

When we get to heaven we won't need faith. Everything we hope for, we'll see face to face. But now we need to develop and use our faith. Being in the fashion industry and at the same time having standards and convictions arouses the curiosity of people who don't know Jesus. Some become curious and ask questions about my faith. Because I am developing and using my faith, God is able to use me as a witness to others.

We need to exercise our faith, moment-to-moment. And by doing so, we can witness to believers and non-believers.

These verses from Hebrews confirm my experience:

> So do not throw away your confidence; it will be richly rewarded. You need to persevere so that when you have done the will of God, you will receive what he has promised. For in just a very little while, "He who

is coming will come and will not delay. But my righteous one will live by faith. And if he shrinks back, I will not be pleased with him." But we are not of those who shrink back and are destroyed, but of those who believe and are saved. (Heb. 10:35–39)

ARE YOU ANSWERING GOD'S CALL AND STEPPING OUT IN FAITH?

For Discussion:

- What is your dream or vision that will take faith in God to happen?
- If there were no limitations, what would you want to achieve in your life?

Meditate on the meaning of these verses:

God called men and women to step out in faith. The following passages describe how some of them were called:

Isaiah 6:8
Esther 4:13–17
Daniel 1:8–17
Luke 1:28–38 (Mary)

And without faith it is impossible to please God, because anyone who comes to him must believe that he exists and that he rewards those who earnestly seek him. (Heb. 11:6)

ALL I NEED

I wanna be who
I am
Can't you see, I'll never be like them
Cause I'm created so unique

Every step I take reflects
who I am in You, Lord
All I need is faith

Small
As a seed

Creation longs for release in the
heavenlies
I got some mountains standing in
my way
But all I gotta do is pray

Pride
Creeps up slowly, carefully
Wraps its arms around me and
Tackles down humility

Deadly is its fragrance, painful is its
bite
And if I take my eyes off You, Lord
I'll lose my sight

So I gotta be
Full of faith
And I gotta be daily
On my face
I will trust in His amazing grace
Every day, every day.

I wanna be who I am
Can't You see I'll never be like them
Cause I'm created so unique
Every step I take
Reflects
Who I am
Who I am in You, Lord.

Chapter 4

Blazing Trail

Discover God's Will for Your Life

God is ready to assume full responsibility for the life wholly yielded to Him.

—Andrew Murray

This is it—this is the one life we have. And what we do with it each day is up to us. When we walk with the Lord, hold His hand, and obey Him, there's no way we can miss His will. One of my favorite passages is "Trust in the LORD with all your heart and lean not on your own understanding; in all your ways acknowledge him, and he will make your paths straight" (Prov. 3:5–6).

Sometimes it's hard to accept God's answers to our prayers—especially when He answers, "Wait" or "No." When God says, "Wait," He may be developing our characters for something better, or protecting us from something harmful. I was disappointed when things didn't work out in New York and wondered what God was doing. Before long He unfolded a new and better opportunity for me. We can't see ahead, but God does, and He will give us the answer that's best for us.

Remember (and be glad) that God is in control of the future. James 4:13–16 tells us, "Now listen, you who say, 'Today or tomorrow we will go to this or that city, spend a year there, carry on business and make money.' Why, you do not even know what will happen tomorrow. What is your life? You are a mist that appears for a little while and then vanishes. Instead, you ought to say, 'If it is the Lord's will, we will live and do this or that.'"

We can and should look for God's will—through prayer, key Bible verses, through the words of a trusted Christian friend.

When God says no to something we want, we may look for the answer *we* want—and we look everywhere. A door opened for me to model in Europe, but I felt God say no. It was hard to refuse that opportunity, but I knew it was not what God wanted for me. We must be careful not to superimpose our desire over God's best answer: "Do not conform any longer to the pattern of this world, but be transformed by the renewing of your mind. Then you will be able to test and approve what God's will is—his good, pleasing and perfect will" (Rom. 12:2).

The above verse states that we must not conform to the world's ways. But with the world constantly telling us to be conformed to garbage, how can we be transformed in our thinking? Renewing our minds comes through meditating on the Bible and asking for God to change our old ways of thinking to match God's way of thinking. Then we will know God's will.

Bible Light

Answers to some of our most important questions can be found in the Bible—questions like "Why am I here?" and "Is there a purpose for my life?" Reading about Jesus' life in the Gospels gives us a picture of what compassion, kindness, strength, courage, love, and wisdom look like. Through Bible study and prayer, God will change us to become more like Him. As I see how much Jesus loves me, I'm inspired—even empowered—to make a difference in my world. I begin to understand that everything about me is unique and that I have a contribution that only I can make.

The motto of the Christian school I attended was, "Your word is a lamp to my feet and a light for my path" (Ps. 119:105). Say you're camping and you use a flashlight at night to walk along a path. You can see only a short distance ahead by the flashlight's beam. You can see enough, however, to stay on the trail and not trip over a rock. God's Word is like that. The Bible doesn't always tell us God's entire plan for our lives, but it does give us everything we need to walk the path that's right in front of us. It tells us to share God's love, to be conformed to Christ, to confess our sins, and it also teaches us practical things for life: don't be "unequally yoked," which means don't marry somebody who doesn't believe like you do (Now we *are* getting awfully practical!); don't lie, cheat, steal, gossip, or sleep around. God has placed those rules there for our protection, to keep us from tripping ourselves up.

The book of Proverbs is a treasure chest of practical things to help us in our everyday lives. It covers subjects like how to control your tongue (12:18) and your temper (15:1), honest work (13:11), being disciplined (15:32), and much more. Following the advice in Proverbs can help you achieve a more successful life. You'll enjoy reading it and you'll grow in wisdom.

The Joshua Principle

Joshua lived about three thousand years ago, and it was his job to defeat the city of Jericho in battle. He turned to God for help, and won the battle. Although the book of Joshua was written many centuries ago, drawing upon his experiences, I've discovered a workable pattern for life in the twenty-first century:

1) **Listen:** Joshua listened and fell on his face (Josh. 5:14).
2) **Obey:** Joshua obeyed what he heard (Josh. 6:2).
3) **See God Move:** God moved and showed His mighty power and the thick walls of Jericho fell down! (Josh. 6:20).

I saw this pattern work in my own life when I was in Atlanta. After prayer and Scripture reading one day, I became excited over a passage that seemed to speak directly to me. In Isaiah, God said, "See, I am doing a new thing! Now it springs up; do you not perceive it?" (43:19). In my own life, I started feeling that the Lord was planning something new for me. I wondered what it could be.

Later in the week, I was reminded that Barbizon Modeling School had been looking for a teacher (Listen). I called them and was told they were hiring that week. I interviewed for the position (Obey) and was hired (God Moved), but not as a teacher—as the education director! This was totally a "God thing."

That God would move this way in my life was amazing! In this job I encouraged girls and guys to develop a more balanced perspective of inner and outer beauty. By doing so they developed a healthier sense of self-worth—one not based upon the reflection in a mirror. The first part of my early dream to minister to teenagers was now coming true!

After about six months, I was offered the position as Director of the International Model and Talent Association (IMTA) at Barbizon/Galaxy Agency. My responsibilities included head-to-

toe imaging: figuring out the best haircut and color, eating plan, exercise plan, makeup colors, and skincare products for each model and actor. I trained the models in runway and print modeling techniques, preparing them to meet agents at competitions, and helping them break into the modeling field. Dale, another instructor, handled the training of the actors—I (with a team of staff) took the students to Los Angeles and New York twice a year. It was an exciting time for me, traveling to big cities, seeing breakthroughs for some of our models, meeting some interesting people, and sharing my faith.

Answered Prayers

One experience in particular made my faith even stronger. We had taken a group of models and actors to the big IMTA competition in Los Angeles. While there, God led me to write a little tract that talked about God's love for each person. It addressed inner versus outer beauty (Listen). I hoped I'd be allowed to hand it out (although some people I worked with had been down on the idea). I felt in my heart, however, that God wanted me to try. So in my hotel room, I prayed, "Lord, if You want these tracts to be handed out, perform one of Your miracles; and Lord, if not, I'll take them back home with me to Atlanta. Please use them wherever You want, and move in power"(Obey).

At the first directors' session, I was surprised to hear a motivational speaker clearly sharing a Christian message. Gene, my boss, leaned over and said to me, "He sounds like you! He should know about your Models for Christ thing." (I had shown the tracts to Gene earlier in the week and asked him if I could hand them out, but he said no).

Now, he leaned over and asked, "Do you have those tracts

with you?" (See God Move). I happened to have a few and passed them to him. He quickly wrote a message and passed the tracts and note to the head of the IMTA. She read the message, looked up, smiled, and wrote a message back. (I felt like I was back in high school passing notes!) She wrote an enthusiastic response, saying we could distribute the tracts! My spirit soared as I saw God's hand at work. I learned that when you *listen* and *obey, God will move.*

Individual Paths

Frequently, we're called to go against the flow, that is, the "normal" ways of the world. I, for instance, felt led by God to enter the modeling field and minister to the young people in that industry. "Normal" teens usually go to college, but I went against the flow. Being perceived as not "normal" has sometimes been difficult to deal with—as difficult as the actual work in the modeling field.

I hadn't anticipated so much pressure to conform to the norm, which insists that the only place to get wisdom is in a college classroom. Don't misunderstand—I'm not discouraging anyone from going to college. In fact, I plan to continue my education. But I now understand what's involved in following God's will rather than the prevailing consensus and I'm determined to please God. "For God did not give us a spirit of timidity, but a spirit of power, of love and of self-discipline" (2 Tim. 1:7).

Moving Forward

Shortly after arriving in Atlanta in 1999, God placed a desire in my heart to start a Models for Christ chapter there. For three months I couldn't find anyone interested in or supportive of the idea, but I continued to pray and trust that God would open this door—in His time. Then I received an e-mail from Christina Nearman, a model in New York. She felt that God had placed the desire in her heart to come to Atlanta and help start a work there. After we exchanged many more e-mails, Christina and her husband, Shane, moved to Atlanta. We formed a team and began a Bible study class for people in the fashion, film, and television industries of Atlanta.

Heavenly Communication

Jesus said, "My sheep listen to my voice; I know them, and they follow me" (John 10:27). Do you recognize and follow His voice? So many voices compete for our attention, but they are the voices of strangers. We must learn to recognize Jesus' voice and tune in to it. Imagine attending a concert. The orchestra has many instruments, but when you choose to focus on the delicate notes of the flute, you can hear them above all the other instruments. God's voice is the song of life, a song that has definite notes and tempos. Ask Him to help you hear His voice above the noisy world. He will teach you to recognize it.

Here are some of the ways God speaks to us:

- An idea or truth in our minds (a revelation like when I realized that I could know God's power in nature but only understand His love through the Bible)
- Circumstances (like when the door shut in New York for me and opened in Atlanta)
- Creation (like when you look at the stars and feel small and understand better how big God is)
- Visions/dreams (like my vision to minister to teens)

- A Godly counselor or friend (like Barbara helping me understand my need for Jesus as Lord of my life)
- A passage in the Bible (like Jeremiah 29:11, which helped me understand that God had a plan for my life). Second Timothy 3:16–17 says, "All Scripture is God-breathed and is useful for teaching, rebuking, correcting and training in righteousness, so that the man of God may be thoroughly equipped for every good work." God's word is the surest indication we have of what God is saying to us. So we can know that any idea, dream, or advice that goes against the Bible's teaching is not from God.

Staying on the Line

We must meet some reasonable conditions in order to hear God's voice. Being receptive to His will for our lives is one condition. Being disobedient or ungrateful can interfere with the line of communication or even cause spiritual deafness. If sin is blocking the reception of God's voice, repent. Tell Him you're sorry for your sins and turn away from them. If you need to forgive someone, be quick to forgive him or her so that unforgiveness doesn't block God's voice.

Think of being receptive in this way: the Devil usually yells his advice; the Holy Spirit whispers. But you can learn to listen. The more you learn about God's character and ways through prayer, Bible study, and discussion with other Christians, the easier it will be for you to recognize His voice.

Matthew 7:7 is another verse that teaches us how to discover God's will: "Ask and it will be given you; seek and you will find; knock and the door will be opened to you." Guess what? God actually *wants* to hear from you. He wants you to share your thoughts and feelings with Him, and He wants you to be specific. Don't ever be afraid to pray—prayer is simply talking to God. Try keeping a journal to help express your desires more clearly and record some of the good things that God is doing in your life.

Fast-Food Expectations

As a fast-food generation, we want everything now—or even yesterday! It's no wonder we get impatient waiting to know God's will for our lives. Just like we go to a drive-thru to get a cheeseburger, we sometimes expect God to toss us a message as we speed by Him on our way to something else. But if God has delayed, He has a reason. He sees the big picture, so learn to trust Him.

Trailblazing

Discovering God's will is similar to blazing a trail. When I was in high school in New Zealand, our class attended a school camp. While hiking, we lost the trail and had to make our way through thick, prickly bushes up a steep, slippery mountain. The force of gravity pulled at me, and it took enormous effort to make a path through the walls of brush in the outback. When you say, "Lord, take my life. I want to know and follow Your will. I want to be a leader and world changer," the Lord may ask you to be a trailblazer. When that happens, He may place you on a steep path that's choked with weeds and brush. You look around and think, "Hello, God? Where is my smooth path on flat ground?"

God may give you a vision, a dream, or an idea that makes for a challenging assignment—one that seems impossible. You can choose two attitudes when blazing a trail:

> **Plan A)** See the assignment as an adventure in faith, a chance to see how faith works, a chance to anticipate with excitement each day's progress, whacking those bushes with the energy God supplies to climb uphill;
>
> **Plan B)** Complain and whine, creep along, dragging your feet up the hill, just waiting for the branches to slap you in the face.

Why not say in your heart today, "Lord, plant this seed, put me in the desert, if You wish. Help me grow into a strong warrior for Jesus." Now go forward, using Plan A!

These words from Isaiah 41:17–20 will help inspire you:

> The poor and needy search for water, but there is none; their tongues are parched with thirst. But I the Lord will answer them; I, the God of Israel, will not forsake them. I will make rivers flow on barren heights, and springs within the valleys. I will turn the desert into pools of water, and the parched ground into springs. I will put in the desert the cedar and the acacia, the myrtle and the olive. I will set pines in the wasteland, the fir and the cypress together, so that people may see and know, may consider and understand, that the hand of the Lord has done this, that the Holy One of Israel has created it.

This picture shows that God can make the desert of our heart bloom with life, too!

IS GOD CALLING YOU TO BE A TRAILBLAZER?

For Discussion:

- How can you become a trailblazer in your school or in other areas of your life?
- Is sin preventing you from clearly hearing God's voice?

Meditate on the meaning of these verses:

> Trust in the LORD with all your heart and lean not on your own understanding; in all your ways acknowledge him, and he will make your paths straight. (Prov. 3:5–6)

> "Love the Lord your God with all your heart and with all your soul and with all your mind." This is the first and greatest commandment. And the second is like it: "Love your neighbor as yourself." (Matt. 22:37–39)

> For we are God's workmanship, created in Christ Jesus to do good works, which God prepared in advance for us to do. (Eph. 2:10)

PRODIGAL ONE

Been on a long journey
Far from my destiny.
Can't take back what I've done

The weight is heavy
can't go dragging it no more.

My ears are straining, Lord
I've tried to hear You, Lord
But something's blocking them.

Must be my sin.
gotta lay it down

At the cross where You died for me.
So You can forgive me.

Your word says unconditionally
And though I stumble and crawl
Your outstretched hand
is a bridge
even when I fall.

I'm so grateful that You
Take me as I am.

I can't live another day
without You
in my life.

The years will pass
And each day I'll have You by my side
'Cause You died for me
You set me free.

You're running to meet me
I see Your arms so wide
A tear runs down Your face
I don't deserve it but You're running
to me!

Chapter 5

Prayer Flame

Set Aside Time for Just You and God

Prayer is like having a cell phone to God. Faith is the batteries. Before I fully understood prayer, I struggled to sit still and talk to Someone who is invisible. But now I understand that prayer is just talking to God, like I'd talk to a friend over the phone.

Just as our cell phones have individual numbers, God knows our individual *spiritual* numbers and recognizes them, like on caller ID: "The LORD is near to all who call on him, to all who call on him in truth" (Ps. 145:18). Even though we can't see God, He waits for our calls and listens to what we say.

Frequent Calling

As I read the New Testament, I'm amazed at how often Jesus set aside special time to pray. He sought the Father for direction and regularly poured His heart out to Him. Whenever Jesus needed His "Daddy," He didn't hesitate to talk to Him in prayer.

How can we get to know a person if we don't talk to or

spend time with him or her? In the same way, it takes time, effort, and dedication to develop a relationship with God. But the rewards are priceless. Sometimes when I start talking to God I'm angry or confused. But by the end of my prayer time, a peace takes over and I come away feeling forgiven and accepted. At other times I feel sad, and pour out my heart to God as my friend. Praying won't feel like a chore once you've experienced its life-giving power. And in very little time, praying will become as natural as brushing your hair.

Sometimes I'm rushed and don't have time to quietly start the day. On those days, I turn off the car radio, turn on my cell prayer-phone, and commit my day to Jesus. You can pray anywhere, anytime, during any activity. The point is, God hears you. We know this because Psalm 4:3 assures us, "The Lord will hear when I call to him."

Earlier, I talked about keeping short accounts with God by quickly confessing our sins. This is especially important when it comes to prayer, because sin can create a barrier between you and God. The Bible says in Psalm 66:18, "If I had cherished sin in my heart, the Lord would not have listened." So, as you begin your prayer, check your heart and confess your sins. Ask God to forgive you, so that He can fulfill His promise and cleanse you.

On occasion, I feel confused and uncertain about what to pray for. God understands and still loves me. If I'm feeling lonely, unpopular, or anxious about my future, I picture myself approaching God's throne, jumping in His lap, and placing all my worries in His capable hands. At those times, these verses are a refuge for me: "Do not be anxious about anything, but in everything, by prayer and petition, with thanksgiving, present your requests to God. And the peace of God, which transcends all understanding, will guard your hearts and your minds in Christ Jesus" (Phil. 4:6–7).

Expanding Your Prayer Life

When I was having problems with acne, my mother and I developed this strategy for prayer: whenever I became over-anxious about my complexion or it threatened to dominate my life, I consciously used these negative feelings as a prompt to pray for someone's salvation. In this way, I turned the focus away from myself and concentrated on doing something good for someone else. My prayers not only blessed another person, but helped me maintain a better perspective about my own problem.

Praying can include fasting—yes, going without food for a time while you seek God. If you're facing a very difficult problem or a crisis, fasting can add power to your prayer, acknowledging your total dependence upon God, and focusing your heart, mind, and soul upon Him. Deuteronomy 4:29–31 says, "If from there you seek the LORD your God, you will find him if you look for him with all your heart and with all your soul. . . . For the LORD your God is a merciful God." Things happen in the invisible, spiritual realm when we fast and pray.

A fast could be going without one meal in a day, or giving up a certain food that you love, like a Snickers candy bar or Doritos chips. If you have diabetes or other nutrition-sensitive health problems, don't fast until you get approval from your doctor. God will understand if you can't fast because of medical reasons.

Pray to Combat Evils

Sometimes it's hard to pray, especially when someone has hurt us or we've experienced a great disappointment. We hurt badly and wonder why God allowed such hurtful things to happen. We wonder, *If God is good, why is there so much suffering in the world?* Remember—pain and suffering began a long time ago, in the Garden of Eden with Adam and Eve. Rather than making us like robots, God chose to give us free will so we could choose to obey or disobey. In the garden, Adam and Eve made a choice to disobey God, and their disobedience allowed sin to enter the world. As a result, we are subject to all types of terrible things including earthquakes, floods, famines, wars, disease, and death.

Satan, as the prince of this world, uses the bad things that happen on earth for his own ends. His goal is to confuse us and make us doubt God's love for us, so he uses disease, catastrophes, and lies to make us question God's goodness and love for us.

We are in a spiritual battle, and to win we must live by faith and by prayer. That means trusting God and turning to Him in prayer even when the circumstances are bad and even impossible to understand. Each time something bad happens to us and we choose to trust God—regardless of the circumstances—and turn it over to Him in prayer, we stop Satan's darts. The next time you face a difficult situation, rather than pray, "Why me, God?" pray, "God, what do You want me to learn from this? What do You want me to do?" Maybe He wants you to be more patient, or kind, or to trust Him even though you don't understand. The important thing is, God is only a prayer away. You will never have to face any problem alone.

Praying for Others

Spiritual intercession is praying for others. Intercessory prayer became very real for me when I was in China on a two-month DTS outreach/mission trip with YWAM. I learned that we have to pray beyond our personal wants and needs and turn our hearts toward the needs of others. We have to care about what

Jesus cares about, and He cares about everyone. In China, I glimpsed the power and timing of prayer while witnessing to Jian, a young Chinese girl (whose name I have changed and whose story I will later describe in more detail).

Shortly after meeting with Jian, my mother asked what had been happening with me. "I had been led to pray for you," she said. "But as I was praying, the Holy Spirit impressed upon me to pray for the person you were witnessing to."

"When did this happen, Mom?" I asked.

We learned that my mom's prompting occurred during the encounter when Jian accepted the Lord! God had allowed us to see the power of intercessory prayer. Wow!

Be Still

When you pray, you can't just talk—you have to listen, too. That means to look expectantly for an answer. It might come through the words of a song, a friend, a quote in a book. Take time to read your Bible, and give God an opportunity to communicate to you through His Word. If a particular Bible verse comes to your mind, for instance, think carefully about it. Think about what it meant to the people in Bible times who heard that message and find what it is saying to you personally in today's world. Place yourself "in" the Bible verse. What is God saying to you? If you listen with expectation, a new dimension of life can open up for you.

If you feel confused and uncertain about the direction that your life is taking and where God is leading you, pray this prayer with me:

> Lord, I am weak. I am scared and feeling fearful about my future. But I'm thankful that, although I am weak,

You are so strong. I ask for the Holy Spirit to fill me with courage and peace. Lord, please give me ears that are tuned to Your voice so I can hear and obey You. I don't have much to give, but I do give You me—all of me. What is Your will, Lord? Show me. Lead me. I believe I was born for a purpose because Your Word says so in Jeremiah 29:11. I pray for an extra dose of patience as I wait for You to reveal—step-by-step—the path You have chosen for me.

Please bind the Enemy's schemes to confuse me and make me impatient. I'm putting on the full armor of God right now: the belt of truth, the breastplate of righteousness, the shoes of peace, the shield of faith, the helmet of salvation, the sword of the Spirit (Eph. 6:14–17).

Protect me, lead me, and ignite the spark within me. Turn it into a blazing fire, a consuming fire of desire to live a life that pleases You and brings honor to Your name. I pray this in Jesus' name. Amen.

SET ASIDE TIME TO PRAY EVERY DAY. MAKE IT A SPECIAL TIME JUST FOR YOU AND GOD.

For Discussion:

- Do you find it difficult to pray?
- When did you last pray?
- Have you ever had a prayer answered?

Meditate on the meaning of these verses:

In the same way, the Spirit helps us in our weakness. We do not know what we ought to pray for, but the Spirit himself intercedes for us with groans that words cannot express. (Rom. 8:26)

Therefore confess your sins to each other and pray for each other so that you may be healed. The prayer of a righteous man is powerful and effective. (James 5:16)

But when you pray, go into your room, close the door and pray to your Father, who is unseen. Then your Father, who sees what is done in secret, will reward you. (Matt. 6:6)

When you ask, you do not receive, because you ask with wrong motives, that you may spend what you get on your pleasures. (James 4:3)

CHANGE

Cotton ball clouds creep by
As I let out a sigh
My life I'm leaving behind
It will never rewind

Rain drops settle on a thirsty ground
Everything seems to come around
Dust has settled in the caverns of my soul
I need You to take control
Wind blows violently
As You convict quietly

Oh Lord my life is in Your hands
Take me, change me, show me Your plans
I need Your love to mend my wounds.

As thunder bolts from the sky
No longer will I live a lie
Your truth has set me free
Yeah

And wind blows violently
And Your love is healing me!

Chapter 6

Fire Spreader

Share the Fire of God That's in Your Life

> Therefore go and make disciples of all nations, baptizing them in the name of the Father and of the Son and of the Holy Spirit, and teaching them to obey everything I have commanded you. And surely I am with you always, to the very end of the age.
>
> Matthew 28:19–20

We didn't know a soul in that Chinese city. Our YWAM team of nine people felt God leading us there, but we'd established no contacts. On the thirty-six-hour train ride into the heart of China, we prayed that the Lord would reveal why we were going there and where we were supposed to stay.

On the train, one of our teammates (who spoke Chinese) met a man who said the university would probably let us stay there. We believed this to be a sign from God and trusted that this was part of God's answer to our prayers.

Answered Prayers

We took taxis to the university, and we found out that we could indeed stay there! When we first walked through the gates wearing our backpacks, people stopped and stared at the Americans. One of the girls came up to us and said, "Hello, how are you?" in English! We were shocked and delighted to learn that the school was a teachers college. The girl, "Jian," was very friendly and I felt an immediate connection with her. I prayed that I would be able to share Christ with her even though we couldn't speak about Jesus in public. The policy of China's communist government forbade it. But Jian was able to come to my room so we could share. Eventually, I got to know her really well.

The Joy of Sharing Faith

During one of Jian's visits I began to share my faith with her, explaining my beliefs. Although we had a little trouble communicating, the Holy Spirit blessed us with understanding. I told her about the spiritual significance of Christmas and Easter and how Jesus died for me—and for her. She had heard of *Esue-Jesus,* and I asked her what she believed.

She said, "I have been taught that there is no God. It is enough that I believe in myself."

She said her parents were communists and that she was being taught Marxism in school. I kept praying in my spirit and telling her how God had given my life purpose and meaning.

She said, "I think I would like to believe, but please ask me questions to make sure I understand."

I asked, "Why do you want to believe in Jesus?"

"Because," she said, "He will give me peace and a purpose in my life and He died for my sins." She understood!

I asked her if she had any questions for me.

"Does Jesus have brothers or sisters?" she asked.

I told her about His birth through the Holy Spirit and being God's Son. She understood.

Many people in China are hostile to Christianity, and I cautioned Jian to be very careful with whom she shared her new faith. I asked her to pray, but only if she understood how difficult it would be for her—a Christian in China.

She wanted to pray and tried to pray in English, but I stopped her. "Pray in Chinese," I said. "God understands Chinese."

I'll never forget the shocked look on her face! She said "No, how can He speak Chinese? How big is this God?"

"God isn't a Western God," I explained. "He died for all the people of the world."

She prayed in Chinese and invited God into her life. While she was praying, I felt God prompting me to lay my hands on her. I did and asked God to speak to her. She was amazed that God might have something to say to her, so we both waited quietly.

After what seemed like years, but was only five minutes, I looked at Jian and she was smiling. I asked her what God had said to her.

"He spoke to me in Chinese," she said, but she had difficulty translating it because the message had been so personal. "Can I pray and talk to Him anywhere?" she asked.

I told her yes and gave her a Bible-on-tape in Chinese and an English Bible. We found a small underground church with eleven members at her university, and she later contacted them.

I still keep in touch with Jian. In one of her letters she said, "I think everyone should believe in Jesus!" She said she often prays for me. God has a plan and a purpose for her too. Praise God!

The Living God Versus Carved Idols

While in China, we visited a Buddhist temple, where the corridor was lined with five hundred life-sized idols of Buddha.

One of the statues represented prosperity and happiness, and people left money there. Worshipers bowed to the statue, praying for answers. Little children as well as elderly people knelt in reverence before that stone god. The sick would rub and touch a large brass pot, hoping for a healing. Mothers brought their sick children and prayed for a cure. Four-year-old children bowed to gold statues, while a hundred elderly women sat on pillows around a large gold Buddha, burning incense and praying. But it was all so empty and without any real hope.

It seems ironic and sad that these Buddhists express faith in carved, lifeless idols that can neither hear nor speak, when the living God—who sees, hears, and knows all people—is ignored. And in the United States, so many people express faith in nothing. It deeply grieves me to think about our complacency toward God's amazing love and mercy.

This experience awakened in me a desire to become a "fire spreader"—one who takes the spark of hope that God offers to those who have never heard the good news of salvation. The religions of the world are very different from Christianity with its good news that Jesus brought to the world. Some people claim that all religions worship the same God, but listen to the way other religions describe their gods, and compare them with the attributes of our God and His Son, Jesus. All gods are not the same.

There is a story about a man who was drowning in the ocean. From the shore, Buddha stood and called out to him, "If you want to save yourself, you must do the following things to make it to shore." Mohammed stood on the shore and said, "It must be Allah's will for you." A Hindu called out, "You can come back a better person in another life." But Jesus waded into the water, swam out, and brought the man safely to shore. This is the God we love and serve!

Ignite the Fire

It's amazing that God uses ordinary people to share His love. None of us is, after all, a perfect Christian; rather we're imperfect people who have been forgiven and renewed in Christ. So you too could become a fire spreader. You don't have to be a biblical scholar to share Christ's love, and being a missionary isn't limited to foreign missions in Africa or China. Your immediate environment is a mission field too. Ask God to show you someone with whom you can share the good news of salvation.

Always pray for people before you talk to them about your faith. Think about your testimony. What do you want to say? It doesn't have to be complicated. Think about how you felt before you asked Christ into your life. What convinced you that you needed the Savior? How is your life better since you made your commitment to Christ Jesus? Be honest about your own life. Be kind and let seekers know that you really care about them. This creates a favorable environment in which faith can ignite and spread.

If you want to experience real joy, share your faith. Matthew 9:37 says, "The harvest is plentiful but the workers are few." The harvest—people that aren't walking with Jesus—is huge, but the workers—Christians who will speak to others about the love of Christ—are few. "Ask the Lord of the harvest, therefore, to send out workers into his harvest field" (Matt. 9:37). Will you ask him to send you?

SPREAD THE FIRE OF GOD TO PEOPLE YOU KNOW. SHARE WHAT GOD IS DOING IN YOUR LIFE.

For Discussion:

- Is something preventing you from openly sharing your faith with others? If yes, what can you do that would enable you to share?
- For practice, share your testimony with a friend.

Meditate on the meaning of these verses:

But you will receive power when the Holy Spirit comes on you; and you will be my witnesses in Jerusalem, and in all Judea and Samaria, and to the ends of the earth. (Acts 1:8)

But in your hearts set apart Christ as Lord. Always be prepared to give an answer to everyone who asks you to give the reason for the hope that you have. But do this with gentleness and respect. (1 Peter 3:15)

ORDINARY

I am ordinary.
Sometimes I wonder what you can do through me.
You used Moses to part the Red Sea,
I know you can use me.

I hold out my hands and I give you my life.
What can you do with me,
Choose me, I will go.

But I'm so ordinary.
I have fears and tears and weaknesses.
Your strength is perfect in these.

I hold out my hands and I give you my life,
What can you do with me,
Choose me, I will go.

Deborah was an ordinary woman,
She was blessed as a leader in the land.
By faith she spoke the words of the Lord,
God was faithful to the end.

I hold out my hands and I give you my life.
What can you with me,
Choose me, I will go!

Photo Album

4 years old, Crater Lake, Oregon

3 years old

Mother and daughter!!

Marjorie and Natalie in Chile

On the farm in New Zealand

Natalie with some of the models going to IMTA in New York

My office at Barbizon in Atlanta

Close friends and Models for Christ
Shane – Christina – Natalie

The Navigators Summer Camp (Barbara in white hat)

YWAM friends preparing to go on outreach to China/India

Chapter 7

Fired-up Warrior

Answer the Call to Be a Warrior

This generation needs to get serious about the Enemy. We need to arm ourselves for spiritual battle, and our equipment is described in Ephesians 6:11–18. It includes a shield, a breastplate, a helmet, a belt, shoes, and even a sword.

The Devil continues to trick us, making us think that wearing only some of the armor is enough. But we must be fully protected so that the Devil's flaming darts cannot get through.

Enlist

The Lord is longing to see His young warriors rise up and say, "Yes, Lord! I want to be a warrior for You." The Lord wants warriors who are willing to train hard, to be as dedicated as those who are in the military or training for the Olympics. So let's get serious and focus our spiritual energy. The apostle Paul encourages us in 1 Corinthians 9:24–27: "Do you not know that in a race all the runners run, but only one gets the prize? Run in such a way as to get the prize. Everyone who competes in the games goes into strict training. They do it to get a crown that will not last; but we do it to get a crown that will last forever. Therefore I do not run like a man running aimlessly; I do not fight like a man beating the air. No, I beat my body and make it my slave so that after I have preached to others, I myself will not be disqualified for the prize."

Give serious thought to this question: Whose warrior do you want to be? We have two choices:

> 1) be drafted and trained by the world as a soldier for the Enemy (Satan); *or*
>
> 2) enlist—and be trained by a loving God for honorable, soul-saving service.

A large segment of our generation is undecided. They spend time and energy struggling somewhere in the middle, sometimes choosing God's way, sometimes the world's way. The Lord is looking for those who'll say, "Yes, Lord! Take me, train me, and use me to be a warrior, fully armed and equipped to make a difference for You."

Training Camp (Basic Course)

Suppose you're a soldier who's enlisted to fight for your country. You're sent to training camp to prepare for battle. In the camp, you train to improve your physical strength. Your body aches from the exercise and push-ups. You attend classes to learn the opposition's weak spots and how to conduct surprise attacks. One of the most important things you'll learn is not to befriend or fraternize with the enemy.

Now suppose you're a soldier for God. Although you are chosen by God to be a warrior, you still must enlist. God won't draft you against your will. As a soldier of God, you're in a war between truth and deception, good and evil. The Lord trains your hands, mind, and soul for spiritual battle (and your heart to do good works). The Enemy, though, uses many weapons and unfair tactics. He offers you the "pleasures" of the world, luring you into his camp, where he can attack you.

But you are not unarmed. God supplies you with weapons that are more powerful than anything the Enemy has. Prayer reinforces and delivers you, the Word of God is the sword that defends you, faith is a shield that protects you. You must take the time to study the Bible and learn about all the weapons and how to use them. And you don't have to be afraid. The Lord promises to be your strength and shield. Ask Him to teach you how to fight and how to win the battle. David says, "He trains my hands for battle; my arms can bend a bow of bronze. . . . You armed me with strength for battle" (2 Sam. 22:35, 40).

Put on your armor and fight. The war between good and evil is dangerous. Compromising with the Enemy, wandering in and out of his territory, puts you at high risk. In this war there are distinct sides. You must choose which side you're on and remain loyal to that side.

The Chart

1) The Opposition—You do not know Christ. You aren't, in fact, interested. You'd be fighting on the world's side.
2) The Undecided—You don't necessarily oppose God *or* the world. This is a dangerous place to be because you are in the middle of the battlefield, a vulnerable target for the Enemy.
3) The Lord's Warriors—You've accepted Christ into your life as your Lord and Savior and have decided that God's ways are better than your ways. You are ready and fully

prepared to be used as a mighty warrior for Christ. You are in the frontlines, being used by God.

4) The Wounded—You know God and have accepted Him into your life, yet allow unresolved hurts, past and present, to hinder your spiritual progress. This prevents you from getting out there on the battlefield. You haven't fully understood God's forgiveness and healing power.

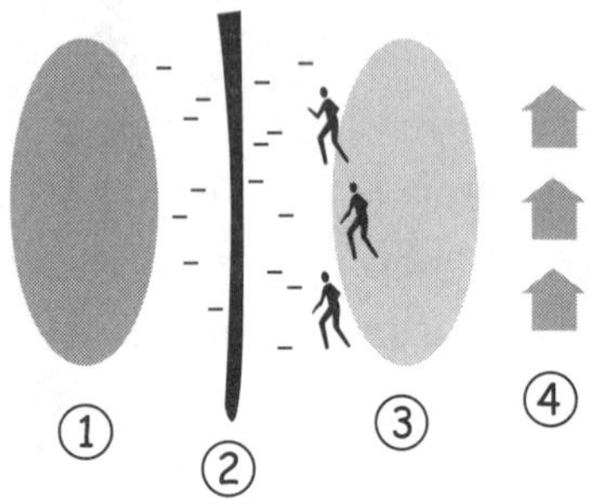

Where are you on this chart? Surely you don't want to fight for the wrong side, wander in the middle of the battlefield, or remain wounded and hurt. God describes our indecision like this: "I know your deeds, that you are neither cold nor hot. I wish you were either one or the other! So, because you are lukewarm—neither hot nor cold—I am about to spit you out of my mouth" (Rev. 3:15–16). This Scripture is intense because the Lord is passionate about His children being on fire.

Instead, accept Jesus as your Savior today. (See chapter 12 if you're not sure how to do that.) If you *are* saved, make a firm commitment to Him, and if you're hurting, let the love of Jesus heal your wounds, even as you prepare for battle.

God's Good Plan

In God's spiritual battle plan, each person is set apart for a specific and unique purpose. No matter how young (or old) you are, it's never too early (or too late) to seek God's will for your life. When I was thirteen years old, God gave me a vision to work with teenagers—to challenge and encourage them to become warriors for Christ. In my journal I wrote a letter to teenagers—although I was barely a teen myself. In the letter, I encouraged teens to stay away from drugs and not to be deceived by the Devil's plans to destroy their lives. Writing this letter was the birth of a continuing mission call, which these years later I now see unfolding.

God has placed a unique character in you and He has a mission for you in His battle plan. Only you can fulfill your mission, because God made you different from every other person alive. Let that fact free you to be *you*, and not compare what God has given you with the gifts and talents of others.

The Warrior's Manual

In order to become a good warrior you need to study God's Word. It's the sword for your armor. God says, "Is not my word like fire . . . and like a hammer that breaks a rock in pieces?" (Jer. 23:29). The Word of God will help you identify the schemes of the Devil. In 1 Peter 5:8–9, for instance, the Devil is described as a roaring lion. He's loud with his doubts, lies, and accusations: "You're only one person. You can't change anything. You're too weak." But you are to "resist him, standing firm in the faith" (1 Peter 5:9a).

Possessing the knowledge of God's Word will make you more effective in every area of your life. It's important to start training *now* because, "the night is nearly over; the day is almost here. So let us put aside the deeds of darkness and put on the armor of light" (Rom. 13:12).

Friends and Family

In the army, your fellow soldiers receive training too, so you can depend upon each other's help in battle: "As iron sharpens iron, so one man sharpens another" (Prov. 27:17). During my teen years, I was blessed to have cousins who were also pursuing God and encouraged me to do so. My brother, Steven, has been a wonderful example, showing me what a kind, generous Christian man looks like.

My dad encouraged me to dream and to follow my dreams, then cheered me on when the going got tough, always believing in me. My mother is a best friend and prayer warrior. Friends of our family prayed for me, encouraged me, and gave me good counsel.

It's important, too, that you carefully choose your friends so that you can challenge and encourage each other while you train for and carry out God's work. In high school I had a close friend, Rose, who was also training to be a warrior for God. We were able to encourage each other to do the right things and say no to the wrong things. Our friendship was like walking on a dark road, each of us holding a candle. Just think how much brighter the light will be on the road you travel when two or three of you walk together! (You can befriend non-Christians too, of course. But your close friends should be believers.) These friends and family are like a pit crew that keeps a race car going in the Daytona 500.

Some of you might not have a supportive family. Your parents might be divorced, too busy, separated, or non-Christian. Maybe life at home is hard and you feel alone in your Christian walk. The good news is that God is on your team. First Peter 5:7 says, "Cast all your anxiety on him because he cares for you." So if you don't have people in your life to help you, ask

God to send special people to love, teach, and encourage you. Talk with a youth leader or trusted adult about getting a mentor in your life.

Although you're young, you don't have to follow the same path that your parents and siblings chose. Your life isn't on a track with its stops and destinations determined by your family's choices. You can make your own choices and become all that *God* has destined for you to become.

Training Camp (Advanced Course)

A lot of training occurs when you're tempted—and you say no to alcohol, drugs, sex, or even gossip. The experiences that confront and test you can actually make you stronger. The Lord is looking for young people who are willing to go through the advanced training and meet the challenge to be different. In some situations, you may find yourself standing alone. Just remember—each time you choose well, the spark within you grows brighter and you become a stronger warrior.

But be careful not to set yourself up for temptation and possible failure. Don't fool yourself into thinking that you can go to a party, knowing that alcohol or drugs will be available, and that somehow you'll be a witness to the people there. That's not the place to make a stand. It's a place to stay away from.

In Christianity, we are saved by grace, and sometimes we take our salvation for granted. We think we can do whatever we want today then ask for forgiveness tomorrow. These verses convict me about the world I see around me: "For, as I have often told you before and now say again even with tears, many live as enemies of the cross of Christ. Their destiny is destruction, their god is their stomach, and their glory is in their shame. Their mind is on earthly things" (Phil. 3:18–19).

Examine yourself and see where you are in this parable:

> The seed is the word of God. Those along the path are the ones who hear, and then the devil comes and takes away the word from their hearts, so that they may not believe and be saved. Those on the rock are the ones who receive the word with joy when they hear it, but they have no root. They believe for a while, but in the time of testing they fall away. The seed that fell among thorns stands for those who hear, but as they go on their way they are choked by life's worries, riches and pleasures, and they do not mature. But the seed on good soil stands for those with a noble and good heart, who hear the word, retain it, and by persevering produce a crop. (Luke 8:11–15)

While in training, allow God to dig up the soil of your heart to prepare good ground. There His Word can take root and grow so you can become a sturdy warrior.

God Holds the Future

Many people try to find out what the future holds. They read astrology columns in magazines and newspapers, consult psychics, and have their palms read. I used to check out the horoscopes in fashion magazines. Then God convicted me that doing so was wrong because I was not trusting in Him. That daily activity could easily have become an idol—something other than God from which to seek direction.

These may seem like harmless activities, but they are part of the occult world (the dark side). Consulting the occult bypasses God and therefore is evil and dangerous. Don't even go there!

When a warrior wants direction for the future, he or she goes to the warrior's manual—the Bible—and in prayer, asks for God's leading.

Like everyone else, I sometimes struggle when making decisions about my future: Should I do something I'm not comfortable with just to look good, to please others and be accepted by them? Not according to Galatians 1:10: "Am I now trying to win the approval of men, or of God? . . . If I were still trying to please men, I would not be a servant of Christ."

Hold Your Position

Going against the flow is hard and takes a lot of guts. The students at your school may look down upon you when you don't join them in activities that would displease God. But if you stick to your biblically-based standards, often those other students will come to respect you. What really matters, though, is that God will be pleased with you.

When I think of the word *warrior*, the following traits come to mind: disciplined, strong, shielded by armor, ready, trained, courageous, focused. There's another aspect to our calling, however: we are to be peace-making warriors too. We've been assigned a position as His ambassadors: "God [is] reconciling the world to himself in Christ. . . . And he has committed to us the message of reconciliation" (2 Cor. 5:19). By showing others the peace that come through salvation in Christ, we're adding numbers of warriors to the ranks!

God wants us to be warriors of purity—to fight through temptations and be good examples, pure and upright as "children of God without fault in a crooked and depraved generation, in which you shine like stars in the universe" (Phil. 2:15).

Be a star!

ANSWER THE CALL TO BE A WARRIOR.

For Discussion:

- Ask God to show you where you are in your warrior training and how to proceed to the next level.
- Describe an experience when the fear of what others might have thought of you affected your choice.
- Where are you on the chart? (p. 82)

Meditate on the meaning of these verses:

For this very reason, make every effort to add to your faith goodness; and to goodness, knowledge; and to knowledge, self-control; and to self-control, perseverance; and to perseverance, godliness; and to godliness, brotherly kindness; and to brotherly kindness, love. For if you possess these qualities in increasing measure, they will keep you from being ineffective and unproductive in your knowledge of our Lord Jesus Christ. (2 Peter 1:5–8)

Go over the picture of the armor of God in Ephesians 6:11–17.

Never forget the secret of your strength. "'Not by might nor by power, but by my Spirit,' says the LORD Almighty" (Zech. 4:6b).

LAY IT DOWN
(Song)

I'm at a loss for words
As I lay it all down
I crumble in Your presence
As Your love sets me free
I consider all a loss
Compared to Your greatness, Oh Lord
I will bow down to You
I will be found in You
I lay it down, I lay it down
Your great love
Like a glistening star
Chases all my fears away
Causes me to rise up and say
I consider all a loss
Compared to Your greatness, Oh Lord
I will bow down to You
I will be found in You
I lay it down, I lay it down.

Chapter 8

Purified Mind

See Things God's Way

I don't want ugly, sinful things to soil my spirit. In this new millennium, we're surrounded by cesspools of violence, sex, and other impurities—in movies, on TV, in magazines. It's easy to become inured and complacent.

"But among you there must not be even a hint of sexual immorality, or of any kind of impurity, or of greed, because these are improper for God's holy people. Nor should there be obscenity, foolish talk or coarse joking, which are out of place, but rather thanksgiving" (Eph. 5:3–4). It's hard to believe that God is even concerned about what we say, but He is. Proverbs 18:21 tells us, "The tongue has the power of life and death." The words that we say—or don't say—are extremely important. They tell others what kind of a person we are.

When I was in school, I listened to gossip about other students. The gossip was usually untrue, but it still hurt the people we gossiped about. The tongue has power (for both good and evil), so we should be very careful when choosing our words.

Ephesians 5:5–11 says:

> For of this you can be sure: No immoral, impure or greedy person—such a man is an idolater—has any

> inheritance in the kingdom of Christ and of God. Let no one deceive you with empty words, for because of such things God's wrath comes on those who are disobedient. Therefore do not be partners with them.
>
> For you were once darkness but now you are light in the Lord. Live as children of light (for the fruit of the light consists in all goodness, righteousness and truth) and find out what pleases the Lord. Have nothing to do with the fruitless deeds of darkness.

I don't want to be a partner with people who choose impure ways over God's ways. The friends we hang out with can influence our choices, so let's be careful who we choose to spend our time with. Let's ask ourselves, *Are we influencing them—or are they influencing us?*

The Lord wants to see warriors of purity who will rise up and say, "No, I'm not going to watch this," or "No, I'm not going to read that." Instead, let's focus on, "whatever is true, whatever is noble, whatever is right, whatever is pure, whatever is lovely, whatever is admirable—if anything is excellent and praiseworthy—think about such things" (Phil. 4:8). The world contains countless good, decent, lovely, and beneficial things to think about. Why waste time and brain cells on junk thoughts? Memorize the above verse and hold it up like a shield when Satan tempts you.

Fiery Darts

The Enemy is attacking purity. Why? Because God cares a lot about purity: "Blessed are the pure in heart, for they will see God" (Matt. 5:8). The Devil is continually assaulting us, trying to twist our thoughts through movies, Web sites, magazines, music, movies, and television.

Marriage, for example, is a relationship blessed by God. The Bible compares marriage to Christ's union with us—the church. No wonder the Devil doesn't want us to take marriage seriously! The lifestyles of many actors and sports heroes mock marriage vows as old fashioned. Society seems to tolerate impure behavior by celebrities, and this looking the other way confuses young people, creating uncertainty about what is right and acceptable.

The Devil wants to deceive us. He wants us to believe that society's norms are morally okay, and accept them as God's way. In our contemporary pop-culture, some people seem to have lost sight of morality. They make immoral decisions, not even realizing how sinful those decisions are. That's why it's important to study the Bible and know what *God* defines as right and wrong.

Like warriors in battle, we must stand up to society's immoral views and standards. We must control our thoughts, what we read, where we go, and what we see. We need God's help to achieve and maintain purity, but hey, He wants to help us. And if we have fallen short of the mark, remember—God will forgive a repentant heart and restore purity.

Spiritual Glasses

Because impurity is so prevalent, you might feel that attaining and maintaining a pure heart is impossible. Imagine that you're wearing a pair of purity glasses (or if you prefer, contact lenses). As you go through your day—at home, at school, at the mall, or the movies—ask God to sharpen your spiritual and practical vision so that you can clearly see what is good and what is evil. Ask God to help you make decisions that will honor Him and keep you safe.

Sometimes, declining to be part of something will require sacrifice, because "everyone else is doing it." But remember, life is short—and every decision counts. A seemingly small decision—like skipping an immoral movie—can have your friends wondering and asking, "Why?" When they ask, you have an opportunity to share your faith with them! They might laugh and be unimpressed, but your decision and action will still have an effect. This is your opportunity to make a difference. You'll be the light in the darkness—which is what God is calling you to be.

Mission Field

"Go into all the world." When I was considering returning to the field of modeling, Mom and I prayed that I would make the right decision. Sure, I enjoyed the glamour of being a model, but more importantly, I really cared for the other girls who were in that career.

While we prayed for protection in an environment with so many temptations and impurities, Mom saw a vision. She saw me in a bubble car like the Pope rides in for protection from the crowds. She saw me, protected as I worked in the modeling field. The Lord was telling her that He would provide protection for me. I would be in the world but definitely not of it. Being in the world but not of it is difficult to achieve and maintain, but with God, all things are possible.

I want to be different, to be pure—to always be a sweet fragrance to God. So daily, even hourly, I willingly confess my areas of weakness and trust Him to protect me and help me say no to temptation. I also ask for strength to continue each day and ask Him to cleanse me when I sin. You need His help too. Ask Him to show you the Enemy's schemes so that you won't be caught off-guard.

Hidden Dangers

Emily, a twelve-year-old who's a friend of our family, shared that she and most of her friends would like to be models. I explained to Emily that it's important to put more of your effort into developing your inner beauty first.

Why? The modeling field can be very superficial and competitive. Sometimes it's a challenge for models to maintain their values, to remain pure and resist the temptation to say yes to a job that compromises their standards. It's hard to actually earn a living from modeling. It's a competitive business, and not many reach the status of supermodels like Kate Moss, Naomi Campbell, or Cindy Crawford. Unethical people know how much young girls want to become famous models, and exploiters in the business will try to mislead young hopefuls, pretending to offer "opportunities," then take advantage of the aspiring models.

Strip away the mask of glamour and you'll find people full of envy, jealousy, loneliness, and insecurity. Oh, how God wants to show Himself to them! And if God leads you to be a light in the fashion industry, He will clearly show you and He will give you the strength necessary.

The Light of Purity

"The night is nearly over; the day is almost here. So let us put aside the deeds of darkness and put on the armor of light" (Rom. 13:12). This armor of light reflects your purity and can actually attract people to you.

Imagine that it's night. You're on an unfamiliar road, and your candle helps you see where you're walking. Other people are walking on the road carrying candles, but only yours is lit. You hear them talking, saying, "Ouch! Watch out; that's my toe!" Since you're not hiding your light, people approach you and ask, "Hey . . . uh . . . how did you get your candle burning? Can I have a light from your candle?" This is your opportunity to share the light of Jesus and reveal God's love to them!

Purity—it sets you apart like a light in the darkness and attracts others to Jesus living within you.

PUT ON YOUR PURITY GLASSES AND ASK GOD TO HELP YOU SEE THINGS HIS WAY!

For Discussion:

- Do things in your life distract you from purity?
- If Jesus hung out with you and your friends for a night, would you feel ashamed or delighted to show Him the things that you do?

Meditate on the meaning of these verses:

> Do not conform any longer to the pattern of this world, but be transformed by the renewing of your mind. (Rom. 12:2)

> Do not let any unwholesome talk come out of your mouths, but only what is helpful for building others up according to their needs, that it may benefit those who listen. (Eph. 4:29)

> Out of the same mouth come praise and cursing. My brothers, this should not be. Can both fresh water and salt water flow from the same spring? (James 3:10–11)

THIS DAY
(Song)

Sitting here thinking of the choices in my life
poured out and scattered in my thoughts
I breathe in and exhale all my worries
'Cause You're in control, and I won't let that go.
Have mercy on me, Oh God
According to Your unfailing love
According to Your great compassion
Wash away my iniquity
Show me all You want for me
Then I can live this day in a new way
Sitting here thinking how He longs to know me more
How often I have turned Him away
Crush the boxes I have placed around me carefully
It brings me to my knees to think of how I need Your reality.

Sitting here thinking of the blessings in my life
How good You've been though I know I don't deserve it
After all You came to earth to reach me
You died for me, I won't forget Your mercy
Not this day I can't forget Your mercy

Sitting here thinking how You long to know me more
I long to know You too. In this day, In this day.

Garden Parable

Imagine that your heart is a garden. When you become a Christian, Jesus builds a fence with a gate for your garden. The soil is rich and moist there, and no weeds, fruits, or flowers grow there yet. All the weeds (sins) that were in there before Jesus entered have been pulled up and thrown into a fire. Now it is a beautiful piece of land with a fence and a gate.

Jesus (the Gardener) prepares the soil to plant the seeds for the flowers and fruit trees that He plans to grow there. The plants and trees are uniquely chosen specifically for your garden. No other garden will be like yours. Jesus takes His time planting your garden and faithfully waters it.

But you have the power to grant access to others. You decide carelessly and randomly what you like and soon you've driven the Gardener to the edge while you take over and redesign your garden. You trust others and listen as they tell you about their flowers and their fruits.

Now, instead of a lovely, private garden, your heart resembles a neglected, littered public park. Weeds sprout up. Too many people are wandering through, trampling your garden. You've

forgotten that your heart even had a Gardener.

He, however, hasn't forgotten. He's waiting for you to realize that your garden is a terrible mess and ask for His help again. When it's so overgrown that you can't even find the gate, you call out, "Are you here? Why has my garden been ruined?"

The Gardener responds, "I wanted to keep it healthy and beautiful for you, but the people you let in prevented Me from accomplishing it. I'll gladly weed and replant your garden, but first you must tell all those people to leave."

"Why?" you ask.

He gently replies, "You cannot have one pulling weeds while others are planting more. I have a special design for your garden, but you must trust Me and do what I ask. In the right season you will see wonderful results. Your garden will grow and bless you and many others with its nourishing fruits and fragrant flowers."

Who's been planting in your garden?

Chapter 9

Burning Desires

Clarify Your Standards About Sex and Dating

Many of us are confused and struggling with our sexuality. And the world presents examples of dating and relationships that confuse us even more. The subject of dating is of major interest to the society we live in, and opinions abound on when to start, who to date, and how intense a dating relationship should be.

In contemporary society the meanings of *love* and *dating* have been distorted and devalued. For many people *love* has come to mean physical feelings, but feelings are temporary. So dating, rather than a time to find out if you could love the other person, has become a game: get as much physical gratification as you can and then move on to the next person to "love."

Part of Christian training, however, consists of learning to have patience. Our willingness to wait for our life-mates gives us time to mature. It's great when someone appreciates you and assures you that you're attractive. But when you play the dating game, things can quickly get intense. Someone may try to take you beyond the point you intended to go.

Standards

It's important to determine where you want to end before you begin. As someone told me once, "Don't just slide, decide." What are some issues you need to consider?

- Will you wait for sex until marriage?
- Will you date only a Christian?
- Will you date only in groups, or date one-on-one?
- Will you tolerate drinking and drug use?
- Will you limit the type of films you'll see to those that aren't full of sex?
- Will you tolerate wandering hands or extended kissing?
- Will you keep your clothes buttoned, snapped, and zipped up?
- Will you discuss your standards with a person before you ever go out with him or her?

Add to or delete from this list to make it your own personal set of standards!

In the dating game, too many people, it seems, try to get what they want out of the other person. Girls tell me that guys say, "I love you," to get sex; I've talked to girls who will give sex to get love. Both are taking advantage of each other. Some people boost their egos by having a trophy date—a handsome guy or a pretty girl for whom they have no real feelings.

In my opinion, such selfish motives aren't what God intends in a relationship. Our hearts and souls are much too valuable to cheapen them by passing them around. Although playing the dating game may seem like the cool thing to do, it's not. For now, I'll get my confidence and appreciation from God, from my family, and from my trusted friends.

I've made a list of the main characteristics I want in a future husband: spiritual depth, personality, and yes—even looks. I've given this list to God in a prayer, and I'm trusting that He will provide the right man—at the right time—for me. In the meantime, I'm busy becoming all that I can be—developing my own interests and tastes, meeting new people and learning to relate to them.

The process of discovering who I am will better prepare me to share my future with someone else. I'll be more mature, better grounded spiritually, and prepared when God's best choice for me says, "Hello, Natalie."

No Thank You

Being in the modeling field, I've had many opportunities to date. Sometimes I want to say yes to a guy, but if he isn't a man of God and a warrior then I don't want to get involved. I don't want to compromise and settle for less than God's best for me. (It would be a lot easier if he had a mark on his forehead that said, "Hi, Natalie. I'm the one!")

I don't want to go on a date simply because I'm asked, and I don't want to be selfish and lead anyone on. The bottom line is this—I want to guard my heart and focus on Jesus, allowing Him to prepare me to be a wife of noble character like the woman described in Proverbs 31: "The heart of her husband trusts in her. . . . Strength and dignity are her clothing, and she smiles at the future" (vv. 11, 25 NASB).

You might ask, "Natalie, if you don't date, how do you expect to find the right one?" I trust that the God who parted the Red Sea can and will, at the right time, reveal the right person to me. I have guy friends now, and we have fun times in groups—hanging out, playing basketball, talking over coffee, going to movies or to the beach. But my relationships with guys right now is outside of the dating game.

A girl at my fashion college made the comment that I was like a nun because I turned down dates. But I don't mind being called a nun if it means that when I do meet my future husband I'll have my whole heart to offer him. I don't want to work through a lot of issues because of broken relationships and bad choices.

What if a popular, drop-dead gorgeous guy or girl asks you out? Why shouldn't you accept the invitation, especially if you two have a lot in common? The only major difference is his or her lack of commitment to God. This guy or girl says, "Sure, I believe in God too." Yet you notice that this person's behavior doesn't line up with his or her words. "But he's [she's] so awesome!" you tell yourself. Are you training to be a warrior for God? Or do you want to spend your time training to be his girl, or her guy?

Sure, I'd like to have a boyfriend now to share things with. I sometimes get lonely, too, especially when nearly everyone I know has a boyfriend. But when we date just to be dating, we risk selling ourselves short by missing out on God's best plan for our future. We can get ourselves into a lot of trouble by spending too much time dating for fun or pouring ourselves into short-term relationships. We might end up neglecting some of our old friends, shelving our schoolwork, or losing sight of our goals.

Guys, here's a hypothetical situation for you: You meet a girl who's into sports. Your heart skips a beat when you see her and, man, you sure get a lot of attention from your buddies when she's with you. She even goes to your church! Why not get serious and have an exclusive relationship with her? One night the two of you are alone at her parents' house. She wants you to touch her in a way that will lead farther than you know you should go. The first time you back off, but eventually the temptation becomes very attractive. Are you training to be a warrior for God? Or are you about to fall into a trap?

And girls, we need to guard not only *our* hearts, but the man's heart as well. We need to ask ourselves, "Are we deliberately trying to snare a man?" As it says, "I find more bitter than death the woman who is a snare, whose heart is a trap and whose hands are chains. The man who pleases God will escape her, but the sinner she will ensnare" (Eccl. 7:26). Yuck! Bad role model. We sure don't want to resemble a woman like that!

Do Unto Others

Guys and girls can help each other maintain a state of purity. Both sexes need God's help—to protect their own purity as well as the purity of the opposite sex. We girls can begin by not teasing with fashion or words. What are our motives, for instance, when we wear provocative clothes? Girls like outfits that are the latest in style, and most look great in them. But is it wise to wear them? Guys, though, are stimulated by what they see, so we girls need to be careful—we don't want to send the wrong message. Sure, I've been guilty of wearing provocative styles, but I'm now convinced that it's wrong and I dress more modestly.

Men, you need to guard girls' hearts by not flirting with us and leading us on. These selfish and immature games keep you from serving God and distract you from your spiritual and academic goals.

Surely we young men and women don't want to deliberately distract each other from focusing on the best life God has planned for us.

Ouch!

"Can a man scoop fire into his lap without his clothes being burned? Can a man walk on hot coals without his feet being scorched?" (Prov. 6:27–28). Indiscriminate dating is like the fire mentioned in this verse. When a breakup occurs in the dating relationship, someone usually gets burned. Have you been in an unhealthy relationship—always together with the other person, neglecting your other interests and your other friends? Have you done things that you now know are wrong? Don't be discouraged. Ask God to forgive you and immediately begin to make changes—changes that you and your future God-given mate can build upon. Declare, "Today is the first day of the rest of my life."

The Physical Relationship

Many young people have asked me, "How far is too far?" Many times, what they really mean is, "How close to having sex is okay?" Is that question, though, in the right spirit? Wouldn't it be better to ask, "How can I honor the other person?"

Whether or not to have premarital sex is an important issue. The answer is, we should wait until we're married to have sex. Why? First of all, our God has our best interests at heart, and He told us to wait: "Marriage should be honored by all, and the marriage bed kept pure" (Heb. 13:4). I can also think of several practical reasons to say no:

- STDs (Sexually Transmitted Diseases)—Some of these include genital herpes, gonorrhea, chlamydia, genital wart virus, and AIDs. You can get one or more of these diseases from having sexual intercourse with multiple partners or even from having sex just one time with just one partner!

Many STDs are incurable and some, like AIDS, can kill you. Some common symptoms of STDs are painful, burning urination; sores or blisters in the genital area; a rash or intense itching; discharge from the penis or vagina. Pregnant women with herpes expose their babies to terrible risk, as herpes is fatal to the majority of infected newborns. Of the babies who survive, half suffer blindness or brain damage.

- You could become pregnant or make someone pregnant. Although some schools teach "safe" sex, statistics show that among teenagers latex condoms have a failure rate of 20 percent. This means that one in five teen couples, using latex condoms as birth control, will be pregnant within one year!
- Premarital sex can seriously affect your emotional health and well-being. In time you may feel invaded, and once you've had sex you can't undo it. Also, a sexual relationship could arouse jealousy and possessiveness, undermining trust between partners, even those who end up marrying one another. If the relationship breaks up, the emotional pain of rejection and humiliation may require professional help to work through.
- It may affect your future marriage relationship. Poor sexual habits can weaken commitment and make trust more difficult.
- You won't have that special *gift* to give that special someone.
- If you get pregnant or make someone pregnant, goals or dreams like attending college and even beginning your career might have to be delayed.
- Having sex with someone does not guarantee that the person loves you or will stay with you. True love is willing to wait. Pressure is not love.

- God says, "The marriage bed [should be] kept pure"(Heb. 13:4). Disobedience interferes with your relationship with God.

First Thessalonians 4:3–7 (TLB) sums it up this way:

> For God wants you to be holy and pure, and to keep clear of all sexual sin so that each of you will marry in holiness and honor—not in lustful passion as the heathen do, in their ignorance of God and his ways. And this also is God's will: that you never cheat in this matter by taking another man's wife, because the Lord will punish you terribly for this, as we have solemnly told you before. For God has not called us to be dirty-minded and full of lust, but to be holy and clean.

God gives us these moral instructions not only to keep us pure, but to protect us from pain. The physical pleasure of sex lasts only for a moment. Is it worth taking so many risks and possibly having to face undesirable consequences?

If you are no longer a virgin, confess and repent, and God will forgive you. Then begin—from that moment—to lay a good foundation of values that will protect you from more unwise decisions. Determine, for instance, not to have sex again until you are married. Determine to take control of your life, to value yourself and steer clear of places, people, and situations that would compromise your commitment.

Answer the Call

God said, "It is not good for the man to be alone. I will make him a helper suitable for him" (Gen. 2:18). One man and one woman, together for life—that's God's original plan. The world wants to follow its own plan, but God's ways are not the world's ways, and God is calling us to be different from the world.

If waiting for that special person gets hard, picture yourself walking through a desert. God is training you and preparing you for the day when in the distance you'll see the one—the love of your life—walking toward you. The time has arrived for the two of you to link hands and hearts, and start sharing your life-journey, loving and enjoying each other. You'll be so glad you waited!

Some of you might ask, "But what if God doesn't have someone for me?" I've asked that question too. If God has a different path for us, He will prepare us for it. He promises, "Seek first his kingdom and his righteousness, and all these things will be given to you as well" (Matt. 6:33).

ASK GOD TO CLARIFY YOUR STANDARDS IN YOUR RELATIONSHIPS WITH THE OPPOSITE SEX.

For Discussion:

- Are your relationships with guys/girls distracting you from serving God?
- What are some practical ways you can guard the hearts of your brothers/sisters?
- What are some standards that you could set for yourself?

Meditate on the meaning of these verses:

> Those who live according to the sinful nature have their minds set on what that nature desires; but those who live in accordance with the Spirit have their minds set on what the Spirit desires. The mind of sinful man is death, but the mind controlled by the Spirit is life and peace. (Rom. 8:5–6)

> Flee the evil desires of youth, and pursue righteousness, faith, love and peace, along with those [your friends] who call on the Lord out of a pure heart. (2 Tim. 2:22)

> You were taught, with regard to your former way of life, to put off your old self, which is being corrupted by its deceitful desires; to be made new in the attitude of your minds; and to put on the new self, created to be like God in true righteousness and holiness. (Eph. 4:22–24)

> Who is going to harm you if you are eager to do good? But even if you should suffer for what is right, [i.e., gossip about you from peers] you are blessed. "Do not fear what they fear; do not be frightened." But in your hearts set apart Christ as Lord. (1 Peter 3:13–15a)

I WILL WAIT

I love you

I love you Jesus

So I will wait

I will trust you my father

Raise my sword—press onward

Push every hindrance aside

Oh, the sand gets hot sometimes

It gets tempting to grab a hand before it's time.

I love you

I love you Jesus

So I will wait

I will trust you my father

I rub my eyes, in the distance I see
A strong silhouette, who could it be?
It's a warrior, with a sword
A strong man who trusts in the Lord.

I love you
I love you Jesus
So I will wait
I will trust you my father

We link arms, throw out our swords
Marching forward in the name of the Lord.
Wait for the Lord
Be strong and take heart
And wait for the Lord

Chapter 10

Kindling Inner Beauty

To Shape Your Looks from the Inside Out, Make Healthy Choices a Way of Life

Remember the wicked witch in Snow White? Every day she peered into her looking glass and said, "Mirror, mirror on the wall, who's the fairest of them all?" She illustrates that a person can look pretty on the outside and still be filled with bitterness, jealousy, pride, and greed on the inside. But God is never fooled: "Man looks at the outward appearance, but the LORD looks at the heart" (1 Sam. 16:7).

The fashion industry fosters a similar obsession with superficial beauty. I have friends who became anorexic so they would be like the skinny models portrayed in glamour photos. Starving yourself and doing endless exercises is a dangerous road to go down. Take a beauty reality check and put outward appearance in proper perspective.

Healthy Perspective

I have to be careful to not focus too much on my appearance. Being in the modeling field, I'm often surrounded by very beautiful girls. I could easily get caught up in appearance, comparing myself to them and feeling inadequate. But outer beauty is only superficial and passes quickly.

The Bible addresses inner beauty versus outer beauty: "Your beauty should not come from outward adornment, such as braided hair and the wearing of gold jewelry and fine clothes. Instead, it should be that of your inner self, the unfading beauty of a gentle and quiet spirit, which is of great worth in God's sight" (1 Peter 3:3–4). I continually seek God's help to develop a gentle and quiet spirit.

Proverbs 31:30 contains a great portrait of a beautiful woman: "Charm is deceptive and beauty is fleeting; but a woman who fears the LORD is to be praised." If your outward appearance reflected your inner self, what would you look like?

A challenge for you guys can be found in Proverbs 3:13–14: "Blessed is the man who finds wisdom, the man who gains understanding, for she [wisdom] is more profitable than silver and yields better returns than gold."

A Healthy Balance

The amount of attention given to inner and outer beauty needs to be balanced. How much time do you spend in front of the mirror compared to how much time you spend reading the Bible, doing things for others, studying for exams, doing household chores?

While we shouldn't become obsessed about our looks, it's good to do the best we can do with what we have. Why? Because if our appearance says, "I don't care about myself," then why should anyone listen to us when we talk about the wonderful things God has done in our lives?

We can't all look like supermodels, but nearly everyone could benefit from regular exercise, a healthier diet, and sufficient sleep. Choosing the right style of clothes will complement our body types; choosing the right hairstyle will complement our faces. (Tips to help with clothes, hair, and makeup are included in the section "Imaging Outside.") Let's do these things and then stop thinking about ourselves!

If you still aren't satisfied with your looks, remember that you were made to be uniquely *you*. Psalm 139:14 says, "I praise you because I am fearfully and wonderfully made." You may not be in control of your facial features, but you can choose the expressions you wear. Like most everyone, you may want to change some things about yourself but can't. Accept them and thank God for them. Those are part of what makes you unique!

The section "Imaging Outside" talks about what we can do for our outer bodies—the part that the world sees. But the next section concentrates on the area of beauty that will last a lifetime—the inner spirit.

Imaging Inside

Get Your Inside in Shape

This world is out of balance. It overemphasizes the outer appearance and, as a result, we often neglect our inner persons. Jesus said, "What goes into a man's mouth does not make him 'unclean,' but what comes out of his mouth, that is what makes him 'unclean.'" (Matt. 15:11). Since our inner selves are more important than what we look like on the outside, it's better to focus on becoming a supermodel on the inside.

Just as we cleanse our bodies and renew them daily with deodorants, lotions, perfumes, and makeup, we can renew and refresh our inner image. As we discipline our body with exercise and healthy eating to help us become and remain strong and attractive, we can and should exercise and nourish our hearts spiritually and emotionally, and strengthen our minds intellectually and academically.

Spiritual Aerobics

Running or other cardiovascular exercise strengthens the heart and lungs, building muscle tissue and stamina. Regularly reading God's Word is exercise that develops spiritual strength and endurance.

Your spiritual exercise program should include reading a chapter from the Bible and applying its lesson to daily life. As you read your Bible, pray about and meditate upon what you read. Keep a journal for writing down your thoughts as God speaks to you through His Spirit. Ask a youth leader, Sunday school teacher, or pastor to serve as a mentor. A mentor is like a personal trainer who motivates and guides your spiritual growth. If you're not self-motivated, study booklets (available at Christian bookstores) will help you maintain your focus. One of my favorite devotionals for teens is by Lorraine Peterson.

Spiritual Weight Training

If you were training for an athletic competition, you'd do sets of resistance exercises. Using free weights or exercise machines, you'd build muscle strength and help your performance. Sometimes you also need to lift weights in the spiritual realm. These weights may come in the form of testing—challenging times to help build your faith muscles. When you're facing temptations or difficult situations, for instance, you're on the spiritual weight machine. These tests can come in many forms: pressure to do drugs, drink, smoke, cheat, sleep with a guy/girl, scream at your parents, disobey God. Lifting the burden with prayer and a good attitude helps you grow stronger spiritually. When you embrace these testing times as opportunities to become spiritually stronger, you'll be cooperating with God to develop your inner self.

Spiritual Toning and Stretching

Don't be afraid to ask God to stretch you and shape you into His character. Ask Him to reveal the areas that are hindering you from being all you are called to be. I've carried grudges against people. Then, in my spiritual exercise program, I discovered through God's Word that I should forgive them. When I obeyed by forgiving them, I found release and was able to be a little kinder and less critical of others. To s-t-r-e-t-c-h your mind, memorize Scripture that relates to your problem areas. Overcoming these areas will take you to new levels of understanding God and yourself.

Spiritual Cleansing

What do you need after exercising? A shower, right? When you're in the shower, though, you don't just stand there. To get your body clean on the outside, you scrub with soap. It's the same for the inside. To be cleansed and renewed on the inside, let God do the scrubbing. Never be afraid to confess your sins. God already knows about them, so pour out your heart to Him. He knows you and hears you, and is waiting for you to repent so He can cleanse you and restore your purity. Let Him wash you and renew your passion to serve Him.

Scripture also washes and refreshes your thoughts so that you can be a sweet fragrance to God and to those around you. When I read 1 Corinthians 13—the "love" chapter—I begin to understand what Jesus' love for me is like: "Love is patient, love is kind, and is not jealous" (NASB), and I feel an overwhelming acceptance by God and a powerful desire to be that way toward others. Read your Bible and memorize, memorize, memorize. The results of your inner grooming will shine through for others to see.

Here's one of my best inner-beauty tips: don't compare yourself to others. Wishing for what others have or wondering if their walk with God is "better" than yours is a waste of time and energy. To God, you are unique and precious, and He is concerned with your individual spiritual growth. As servants of Christ, our Lord and Master, each of us is accountable to Him, and to Him alone. Don't let jealousy or envy eat away at your inner beauty.

Focus on "whatever is true, whatever is noble, whatever is right, whatever is pure, whatever is lovely, whatever is admirable—if anything is excellent or praiseworthy—think about such things" (Phil. 4:8).

HOW WILL YOU BEGIN TO SHAPE YOUR LOOKS INSIDE?

For Discussion:

- Are you being influenced by what the media—magazines, movies, TV—considers the "ideal" appearance? How?
- Make a plan for your spiritual exercise.

Meditate on the meaning of these verses:

> Do not think of yourself more highly [or lowly] than you ought, but rather think of yourself with sober judgment, in accordance with the measure of faith God has given you. (Rom. 12:3)

> Do you not know that your body is a temple of the Holy Spirit, who is in you, whom you have received from God? You are not your own; you were bought at a price. Therefore honor God with your body. (1 Cor. 6:19–20)

What Is Beauty?

Is Beauty <u>This</u>?

Clear Skin?......Attractive Body?
6 pack abs?........Ripped?
Tall and Slim?........Sexy?

These are EXTERNAL qualities!

This "beautiful" person could
be inwardly feeling:

Insecure........Lonely
Inferior........Arrogant
Afraid of Rejection........Selfish
Jealous........Competitive

Is THIS Beauty?

beauty?

When you look in the mirror,
Do you like what you see?
Most of us have some things we
Like and some things we'd like to
change.
But picture this:
You are inside out and now
Your "inner self" (heart, attitude,
Fears, and thoughts) is
Visible to everyone.
You are inside out!
Did you know that this is
The way God sees us?

First Samuel 16:7 says, "Man looks
at the outer appearance,
but the Lord looks at the heart."

Are you grooming your "inner self,"
Or do you just think about your
Outer appearance?

Imaging Outside

Make Healthy Choices

You are what you eat—it's more than a cliché. Your body is the Spirit's holy temple, so it's important to take good physical care of yourself. You're familiar with the input-output principle: trash in–trash out. Just as what you feed your mind affects your inner beauty, what you feed your body affects your outer beauty. Healthy eating goes a long way toward keeping your hair shiny, your complexion clear, and your energy level up.

Taking good physical care of yourself not only improves your outer appearance; it also affects your inner beauty. Treating your body well shows that you respect yourself. Making healthy eating choices and exercising regularly makes you feel good about yourself.

Eating Habits

A model has to watch what she or he eats, and exercise to stay in shape. Being skinny (for a female) or having huge muscles (for a male) is not the goal. Rather, the goal is to stay in shape and be healthy in order to feel good physically and not have to think about yourself all the time.

When we're in school, it's easy to fall into the habit of eating cafeteria food or grabbing a bag of burgers and fries after school. It's okay to eat like this once in a while. But eating a greasy, fried-food diet too long makes you feel tired, your hair and complexion may not look as nice, and you may gain unwanted pounds.

Make a pact with your friends to eat healthier foods and keep each other accountable. Maximize the fruits and vegetables—minimize the fried foods, fast foods, and desserts.

Balance is the key word in diet—everything in moderation. Here are some other ideas for healthy eating habits.

Morning: Drinking water helps detoxify the body. Start your day with a glass or two of water; a squeeze of lemon juice adds a refreshing taste. Have whole grain cereal with just a little sugar, whole-wheat toast, and yogurt—or an egg and toast. Or enjoy a healthy drink like a fresh or frozen fruit smoothie made with plain yogurt, one or two tablespoons of wheat germ, a dash of flax seed, a teaspoon of honey, and some protein powder for good measure. It's delicious, healthy, and easy to make!

At 10 a.m. and 3 p.m. have fresh fruit or some raw nuts for a snack.

Read the labels on processed foods, checking for hidden sugar. Some other names for sugar are dextrose, glucose, fructose, and malt-dextrin.

Lunch: Whole grain bread with tomato, lettuce, luncheon meat, or cheese; carrot and celery sticks with a dip. A good dip recipe is plain yogurt with tofu and spices. Cottage cheese or humus also makes a good dip.

Dinner: Salad; 3 ounces of broiled, steamed, or baked fish, chicken, or beef; steamed or fresh vegetables; half cup of brown rice. You can substitute pasta as your meal occasionally. Don't use a lot of salt and no MSG (monosodium glutamate—it causes water retention). Use lots of garlic and onions in your cooking as they flavor and are natural antibiotics. A good salad dressing recipe is 2/3-cup extra virgin olive oil; 1/2-cup fresh lemon; garlic and spices to taste. Shake well and refrigerate.

Water—drink, drink, drink. You should have 8 to 9 eight-ounce glasses of water daily to help keep your skin moisturized and detoxify the body.

What would you like to change about your appearance? If there are things you can and want to change, go ahead. A new hairstyle or a new approach to makeup application can emphasize or de-emphasize certain facial features, making a significant difference. A good beauty-advice Web site is www.beautyguru.com.

When I took aspiring models/actors (both guys and girls) to Los Angeles and New York, we would have image consulting sessions. During the sessions, we would cover everything from head to toe: hairstyles, hair color, skincare, diet, exercise, and natural makeup application. I've seen some amazing changes in people when they take care of their bodies by eating right and exercising. One girl I worked with cut out extra snacks and exercised regularly (really working up a sweat), which dramatically toned her body. I saw many of the guys and girls gain more confidence in themselves as they took care of their bodies. They felt more energy, and the discipline helped them realize they could achieve the goals they set.

I wish I could meet one-on-one with each person reading this book. I would love to help you with your personal checklist. Since that's not possible, here are some areas you and your friends could cover in a session. (Some of this applies more to girls than to boys!)

- What hair cuts/colors compliment your facial features? A book that is full of good suggestions, including hair cuts/colors and skincare/makeup is *Beauty, the New Basics* by Rona Berg.
- Experiment with natural, earth tone shades of makeup to see which looks best on you. (Guys can skip this paragraph!)

When you're experimenting with a foundation/cover-up, try a few on the side of one cheek in natural light. The color that blends in is the one you want. My favorite beauty product is Revlon's colorstay concealer.

I usually don't wear foundation unless it's a special event. I just cover any blemishes with my cover-up and put on some blush or bronzing powder. You could play with brown and rosy shades, which are generally good colors for blush. Experiment with different kinds of lip-gloss and colors that you like. Highlight your eyes with a hint of black or brown mascara and eyeliner. Natural colors are usually better, because people want to see *you*, not the makeup. A good resource for makeup tips is *Teenage Beauty* by Bobbi Brown and Annemarie Iversons.

• Always cleanse and moisturize your face morning and night. It's important—even for teens—to use an eye cream, too, as the skin around our eyes is more delicate than the rest of the face. My personal favorites are Cetephil face cleansers and Neutrogena moisturizers and eye cream. If you have questions about a product or ingredient ask your dermatologist.

Once a week, deep cleanse your skin using a facial mask or exfoliant. You can also try steaming by filling a pan with water and one teaspoon of dill seed and bring to a boil. Remove the water from the heat, drape a towel over your head like a tent, and put your face over the steam for five to ten minutes. Splash cold water over your face afterward to close the pores.

• For those of you who experience frequent acne breakouts, experiment with various over-the-counter medications to determine what works best for you, and/or see a dermatologist. If you do have a pimple, put 99 percent isopropyl alcohol on a Q-tip and dab the center of the pimple. It should dry the pimple in a short time. Drinking more water and exercising also can help improve your complexion.

Fire Up Your Body

Plan a fitness program. You don't have to go to a gym. Fast walk, run, or bike for thirty to sixty minutes, three or four times a week. Instead of making you tired, regular, moderate exercise will actually bring up your energy levels. Include some sit-ups, as well as hip and arm strengthening and toning exercises. Tip: cans of soup make good dumbbells for toning arms. If you've never done exercises before, get some advice from a gym or a fitness trainer. Performing exercises improperly is inefficient and can cause injury.

MAKE EATING HEALTHY AND REGULAR EXERCISE A WAY OF LIFE, JUST LIKE BRUSHING YOUR TEETH.

For Discussion:

- How do you plan on developing better eating habits?
- What is your exercise plan?

Meditate on the meaning of these verses:

> For God did not give us a spirit of timidity, but a spirit of power, of love and of self-discipline. (2 Tim. 1:7)

> Let us throw off everything that hinders and the sin that so easily entangles, and let us run with perseverance the race marked out for us. (Heb. 12:1)

Chapter 11

Luminous with Hope

Shine Hope into Your World

Many young people are hurting. Whether they are troubled at home, troubled at school, troubled by insecurities and fears, these young people are gripped by bitterness and pain. They store up the anger, resentment, and hurt until they have no hope.

And the more these young people let their emotions control them, the deeper their hopelessness gets. Desperate to stand on their own, they try to find hope themselves, but don't succeed. The hopelessness hardens their hearts and turns to rage. These troubled young people become the puppets of their emotions, and in their despair, they end up doing desperate things—like shooting others.

My generation is searching for hope, but they are missing God's way of getting them there. It's not possible to find true hope without Jesus. But Christians who, through trials, allow God to soften them to see God's love in the hard things. We can become more compassionate and patient as we continue to place our trust in God.

> For because of our faith, he has brought us into this place of highest privilege where we now stand, and we confidently and joyfully look forward to actually

> becoming all that God has had in mind for us to be. (Rom. 5:2 TLB)

God wants us to be luminous with hope. He means for us to have an abundant life. If only my generation could see God's bigger purpose in everything, life would be such an adventure.

I received an e-mail that filled my heart with renewed hope for my generation. Jayson is from Littleton, Colorado, and he writes,

> Regarding the Columbine High School shooting, I asked God, "Why do bad things happen?" and as much as I wanted a straight-forward answer from God, I didn't get one. And I know I won't. But I did get something. I got a feeling deep down in my heart that said, "This shouldn't happen, and with God's help I can do something about it."
>
> I have the ability to change the world. God said that with faith, I can move mountains, and I have some mountains to move! I have no idea how to solve this problem [of kids becoming filled with such rage]. I have no idea what has gone wrong in the heads of so many of my generation, and I don't know how to stop it, but I am sure going to try.
>
> I don't know *how* I am supposed to change the world, but I will *try* to find out what God's will is for me—and do it. I am not going to stand by any longer and watch my generation flush itself down the toilet.
>
> I am making a vow to myself to take a stand, to make a difference, and I pray I am not alone.

Our world isn't going to change because of new laws or new governments. Our world is going to change when our hearts are changed. My generation needs to rise up and be counted by having a heart transplant. If young people (or anyone for that matter) would open their hearts to the great love of Jesus, which brings such joy, they could find the purpose that Christ brings to their lives. Then, regardless of their present situations, they could walk toward their future, filled with hope.

Yes, this world is hurting, but we can make a difference. We can start by letting Jesus take over our lives and then start spreading that love to our families, friends, schools, communities, and world. Let's make a vow with Jayson. Let's show the world that we care. Let's do something.

Please, join me in a prayer, a cry to God to come and bring revival to this generation:

> Lord Jesus, thank You that You hear our prayers and cries. I pray that You would begin to spark hope in my generation—hope that doesn't come from people or from momentary pleasures, but from God, who is the only sure Hope for all of us. Lord, help me to be bold in sharing this hope with my friends. Lord, surround me with a hedge of protection so that I can stand strong and be a true witness to others who are constantly looking at me. Lord Jesus, bring back hope into this generation. Thank you in advance for hearing our cry and for moving in power. In Jesus' name, Amen.

"May the God of hope fill you with all joy and peace as you trust in him, so that you may overflow with hope by the power of the Holy Spirit" (Rom. 15:13).

AM I BRINGING HOPE TO THE WORLD AROUND ME?

For Discussion:

- Name three things you can do to make a difference in your world.
- What are some simple things you can do to spread kindness, love, and hope in your world?

Meditate on the meaning of these verses:

I have told you these things, so that in me you may have peace. In this world you will have trouble. But take heart! I have overcome the world. (John 16:33)

And hope does not disappoint us, because God has poured out his love into our hearts by the Holy Spirit, whom he has given us. (Rom. 5:5)

May the God of hope fill you with all joy and peace as you trust in him, so that you may overflow with hope by the power of the Holy Spirit. (Rom. 15:13)

RISE UP

RISE UP generation
RISE UP to the call
Voices echo in your soul
Will you RISE UP to the call?

To be Holy—To be Righteous—To be Faithful—
Will you hear it, it's your choice.

Oh let the fire be released
Oh let the floodgates open wide
Pour out your spirit on our land
With your mighty hand.

Set us apart Oh Lord.
Let us shine bright in the dark.
RISE UP generation, RISE UP to the call!

Chapter 12

Steps to Salvation

Light the Spark in Your Life

Most of you probably know about the Bible. You've probably read it or at least heard about it. You probably know that Christmas and Easter are religious holidays. But many people (even some Christians) celebrate them without fully understanding their significance. Santa Claus and the Easter Bunny have cluttered these holy days, and some people never think much beyond these secular images. Christmas and Easter, though, are special. They mark the birth (Christmas) and resurrection (Easter) of Jesus Christ. His life on earth is recorded in the Bible.

Imagine that you've traveled back in time and are standing at the foot of the cross. Jesus' execution is not merely a religious story. It really happened and it has meaning for you. The rest of this chapter explains why Jesus' birth and death hold meaning for you. But for now, imagine you are there at the cross, looking up at Jesus. He is looking at you, and He is dying for you. He is sacrificing His life for your sins; His love and forgiveness cleanse you and bring new life to you. Jesus died on that cross, but He rose from the dead. He is alive in heaven, seated at the right hand of God.

The Love of God

It's part of being human. People need to believe in something bigger than themselves. God put that feeling into people, but most people put their faith into the wrong things. Some people look for aliens to come to earth and rule the world or take them to a faraway galaxy. Others put their faith in false gods or even set themselves up as their own gods.

These people miss the fact—or ignore it—that the Savior, the very Creator of the earth, has already come! The Bible says, "He was in the world, and the world was made through Him, and the world did not know Him" (John 1:10 NKJV). The following story helps to explain this verse:

It was Christmas Eve. Jack's parents had gone to church, but he didn't want anything to do with church. Jack was watching television when he heard a noise outside. He opened the front door, and light from the house beamed out onto the snow-covered lawn.

Much to his surprise he saw some little birds in the yard. He knew they'd die if they stayed out in the cold. Jack tried to get near to them so he could pick them up and put them in the barn. But every time he got close, he cast his shadow over them and they hopped out of reach. He thought, *If only I could become a little bird, I'd tell them, "I've come out here to save you from the cold, not to do you harm."*

But he was too big and different from them, and they wouldn't let him get close enough to save them. Just then the church bells rang and, suddenly, Jack realized *who* Jesus Christ was. He understood that if God had come in all his hugeness, we too would have run away in fear like the little birds hopped away from Jack. Jesus became one of us so that we could hear His message of love and forgiveness.

The Bible tells us, "And the Word [Jesus] became flesh and dwelt among us" (John 1:14 NKJV). While other religions focus on man trying to reach God, Christianity focuses on God reaching down to us.

You've probably heard the old saying, "Don't tell me that you love me. Show me!" That's exactly what God did. John 3:16 is a familiar verse, but read it again and let the love and truth of it touch you anew: "For God so loved the world [that's you] that he gave his one and only Son, that whoever believes in him shall not perish but have eternal life."

God loves us so much that He gave the thing most precious to Him—His Son, Jesus. And Jesus willingly opened His arms wide on the cross and died for us, making it possible for us to become children of the living God.

Think of planting a seed: planting that one seed (Jesus) gave God a harvest of children (us).

All Have Sinned

A lot of people wonder why we need a Savior. Romans 3:23 tells us, "All have sinned and fall short of the glory of God." Because of our sin, we are separated from God. Sin basically is not caring about God, ignoring His way of doing things. Sin is wanting and doing things our way instead of God's way.

I think that all of us recognize that we're sinners. We often do, say, and think terrible things. Sin prevents us from having a relationship with God, so we need cleansing and forgiveness. Sin deserves death, but we can do nothing within our own strength to save ourselves from the penalty of sin. Because we can't save ourselves, God sent Jesus to pay for our salvation through His death on the cross. Our salvation cost Jesus His life, but it's a free gift to us. To receive it, though, we have to open our hearts and accept it.

We can wear a mask and pretend we're good. We can even do a lot of good things, but still have a heart that hasn't been forgiven, cleansed, and changed. Think of it like this: you can learn the Chinese language, you can wear Chinese clothes, but you won't be Chinese unless you are born of Chinese parents. It's the same with becoming a Christian. You can speak the language of God and can put on a godly appearance, but you won't be a child of God unless you are "born" of Jesus Christ, accepting Him as your Savior.

Becoming a Christian, then, is like being "reborn," through a change of heart. And it happens from the inside out, not the other way around: "I have been crucified with Christ and I no longer live, but Christ lives in me. The life I live in the body, I live by faith in the Son of God, who loved me and gave himself for me" (Gal. 2:20).

Through His Son, Jesus, God provides a way for us to know Him, to be forgiven of our sin, and to have eternal life. "Here I am! I stand at the door and knock. If anyone hears my voice and opens the door, I will come in and eat with him, and he with me" (Rev. 3:20). Wow! What an amazing thing.

Jesus lived and walked on this earth. He is not a character in a fairy tale. He was not just a good man or a prophet. He is the Son of God and He died on the cross and rose again. He Lives!

Invitation

Maybe you've never accepted Christ. Perhaps you know about Him, but haven't taken that final step of making Him the Lord of your life.

Imagine that you take your car to the mechanic for repairs.

You say to the mechanic, "Please fix my car, but don't touch the motor." How could the mechanic fix your car? We put God in a similar position. We say, "Here's a problem. I want You to solve it for me," or "Here's a crisis and I'm desperate for You to fix it, *but don't bother those other things in my life.*"

To call Him *Lord* means letting Him have full control of your life. Some people are afraid to do this. But don't be afraid. God loves you and has a good plan for your life. If you feel that God isn't real in your life, it could be because you haven't given Him your whole heart.

If you realize that you need God and you want to have an intimate relationship with Him, pray this simple prayer:

> God, I realize that I am a sinner. I need You to cleanse me and make me pure. Please forgive me for the wrong things that I have done. Forgive me for the good things I should have done for others and didn't. I believe that Jesus died on the cross for me so that I might live abundantly and have eternal life. I believe that Jesus paid a great price for my sin and will cleanse me and make me as white as snow. Thanks for doing this for me. Come and change me and reveal Your love to me. I want You to be in control of my life. In Jesus' name, Amen.

Bringing God into your heart is the beginning of a new life. And God has a plan and a purpose for that life. To fulfill that purpose, He can open doors and create opportunities for you as you embrace His Word and live for Him.

If you aren't ready to accept Christ right now, ask God to reveal Himself to you. It's better to know what you really believe and why. But don't be fooled into thinking that because you're young you have a long time to make a decision about salvation. You never know what might happen. You might not have a second chance! I was sixteen years old when the brother of a friend died. He was hiking with a group, and they went out on a platform to look at the view. The platform collapsed, killing most of them and seriously injuring others. The kids my age all considered ourselves too young to die. This tragedy was a big wake-up call!

I encourage you to read the Gospels (Matthew, Mark, Luke, and John) to learn more about Jesus' life. After accepting Jesus into your life, it's important to get acquainted with other Christians who will encourage you in your faith. Ask other young people about a church that has a good youth program. Most youth programs provide a support system as well as fun and adventurous things to do, like going on mission trips to other states or even other countries.

HAS THE SPARK OF FAITH BEEN LIT IN YOUR LIFE?

For Discussion:

- Have there been times when you've felt a need for God?
- What's preventing you from daily living your life for Him?
- Has the spark in your heart burned with compassion for someone who is hurting? Share with friends experiences you've had or describe them in your journal.

Meditate on the meaning of these verses:

> That if you confess with your mouth, "Jesus is Lord," and believe in your heart that God raised him from the

dead, you will be saved. For it is with your heart that you believe and are justified, and it is with your mouth that you confess and are saved. (Rom. 10:9–10)

Therefore, if anyone is in Christ, he is a new creation; the old has gone, the new has come! (2 Cor. 5:17)

Therefore, there is now no condemnation for those who are in Christ Jesus, because through Christ Jesus the law of the Spirit of life set me free from the law of sin and death. (Rom. 8:1–2)

MY EYES DECEIVE ME

Though a flowing river may dry up
Your love is ever running,
You fill my cup
And though the wind may
Cause the sea to churn and roll
Your words can calm the storm in my heart

My eyes often deceive me
My heart can sometimes be fooled
But when I trust
In Your unfailing love
Your peace and direction
Flow from above

When trials and hardships come my way
It seems like the light around
Grows dim
But Jesus
You
Wrap me in Your arms
And show me there's more You want from me

Though my heart may skip a beat
At things to come
Truth is You're always
Beside me so
Why
Do these doubting thoughts come?

Chapter 13

Youth on Fire

Rise Up and Catch the Fire

I hope that we will wake up. We need to practice obedience to God. We need to give to others and serve others. We need to be a light for those believers whose flame is flickering, and for unbelievers who are groping in darkness. This is an urgent matter because the Lord could return at any time. The Lord is calling us to rise up from our insulated and comfortable places, and to become the warriors He has called us to be.

It's not enough just to believe. I meet many teenagers who say they believe, but their lives reflect little understanding of God's Word and His ways. Jesus isn't in control of their lives. Peter said, "Prepare your minds for action; be self-controlled; set your hope fully on the grace to be given you" (1 Peter 1:13).

The following testimonies come from young people who are on fire. They share their answers to the following questions:

- What do you believe God is calling this generation to do?
- Why did you decide to move beyond complacency and ignite the fire?

Zach Unger, seventeen years old, Sumner, New Zealand

I was born in Haiti, which is a country under satanic influence. I was adopted when I was three by a Canadian family and moved to New Zealand. I considered myself a Christian but never "felt" like a Christian until I took a mission trip back to Haiti. While there, I experienced the power of God and realized His calling on my life.

I feel it's up to us to change our generation. I'd like to see more active spiritual commitment, and I guess it starts with me.

Torrey Moe, nineteen years old, California, USA

This generation has a lot of opportunities and abilities. God has a plan for every single one of us, and those who refuse to believe it will have a very dry relationship with their Lord and Savior, Jesus Christ. Ecclesiastes 3:7 says there is "a time to keep silent and a time to speak." The time to speak is now. We have been silent too long. Our walk must match our talk.

I decided to be on fire for Christ instead of being complacent because I believe and trust that the message of the gospel of Jesus Christ is true. If a person truly believes this, how can that person do anything but completely give herself or himself to Jesus Christ?

Anne Heins, nineteen years old, Sumner, New Zealand

My parents immigrated from Germany to New Zealand and always taught us good values. I'd believed in God, but I thought becoming a Christian would mean giving up everything fun and becoming a judgmental bore. I met some funky, fun girls who loved Jesus and life and then I wanted to find out more about Jesus. Now I want to live my faith and show people that being a Christian isn't a ritual but an adventure.

Living life for God is so much better than living just for yourself. My generation is letting this world dictate what will make them happy, and what this world has to say is just a big lie.

Becca Parrish, twelve years old, Georgia, USA

My testimony is short because I'm twelve, but I'm passionate about my Lord and Savior. Since my father is a Baptist minister, I've been in church all of my life. There's never been a time when I didn't love God or a time when I didn't know that God loved me.

At a young age I realized that just knowing about God wasn't enough. So, when I was nine, I accepted Jesus as my Lord and Savior and gave my heart to Him. So now I have a personal relationship with Christ.

Since then I've tried to show the love of Jesus wherever I am, at church and at school with my friends. I know that younger kids are always watching older kids, so I always want to set the right example by showing them Jesus' love.

Matt Lawrence, seventeen years old, Darfield, New Zealand

I was reared in a Christian home, accepted God as my personal Savior, declared it publicly through baptism, and have been involved in a short-term mission trip. These events solidified my stand for God. Being a sole Christian at my school has both challenged and strengthened my faith.

After many bad experiences with females, I finally feel that God has shown me how to conduct myself in this area of my life. Now God is calling me to do something more about the youth of this generation who are pursuing unwise relationships.

I've chosen to follow God's will and be on fire for Him. I was led to this decision as I observed other males my age flirting and doing things I remember doing. I'm saddened that I wasted my time and energy on those things. However, those experiences were fundamental lessons for me, as God showed me—through my conscience—His will concerning relationships.

Jessie Lysiak, fifteen years old, Georgia, USA

God has been showing me a mental picture of groups of teenagers who spread out all over the world. As teenagers speak to others about the Word of God, they will become examples to people of all ages. God has shown me that through the youth of today, He can change the people of tomorrow. I feel that God is personally calling me to be a prophet of this generation, sent out to be an example through my words and actions, not one of those who defies God by being a "Christian" only on Sunday.

There was a time when I was complacent in my relationship with God and satisfied not to be growing spiritually. Then God sent someone who inspired me to call out to Him and have a daily devotion with Him. Everything has changed, and now I am on fire for God!

Jacob Vargo, eighteen years old, Christchurch, New Zealand

The biggest call for this generation (myself included) is to "church" the un-churched and have a gigantic heart and passion for those who are unsaved. This passion for the lost comes by spending time with God and worshiping Him.

It was only by God's Love that I have the fire and the yearning to do what He wants. He's given me the drive and passion to be the best I can be. It is God at work in me and through me.

"I can do all things through Christ who strengthens me" (Phil. 4:13).

Yasmin McGrane, seventeen years old, Christchurch, New Zealand

God is calling young warriors of this generation to rise up and be shining examples and witnesses to those of our generation who don't know Him. In a world of perversity and complacency, we need to stand for a life of love, purity, and Christian action.

Sitting on the fence was not an option for me. I don't want the image of Christ that I portray to be one of compromise and hypocrisy. I have developed a personal relationship with Him and can not just walk away from such a deep love. When you truly know God, being passionate about Him isn't hard.

****

These testimonies show that some members of this generation are already standing up and being counted. You might like to join their ranks. You could start by mentoring someone younger than you.

People are looking for meaning, purpose, adventure, and a reason to make life worth living. Jesus' great command is, "Love the Lord your God with all your heart and with all your soul and with all your mind" (Matt. 22:37). The adventure starts here. Won't you become a warrior for God?

You can be the spark in a dry field, the spark that ignites the fire in this generation. To see change we must pray and, like Joshua, *listen, obey,* and *see God move!* The examples and testimonies in this book show that prayer is powerful. It's the phone line to God.

Let's pray for revival, for God to come down with His fire, a fire that brings conviction, purity, hope, truth, healing, and true worship. This revival has to start with each of us—individually. Let's listen to His voice and His words of truth in the Bible. Let's do what God tells us even when it's inconvenient, even if we don't feel like it. Only then will we see God move in power.

Daniel stood out in his generation. This was his prayer:

> Now, our God, hear the prayers and petitions of your servant. For your sake O Lord, look with favor on your desolate sanctuary. Give ear, O God, and hear; open

> your eyes and see the desolation of the city that bears your Name. We do not make requests of you because we are righteous, but because of your great mercy. O Lord, listen! O Lord forgive! O Lord, hear and act! For your sake, O my God, do not delay, because your city and your people bear your Name. (Dan. 9:17–19)

Will you stand out in your generation?

Pray with me:

> Thank you, Lord, for Your love of all people and Your desire that we know You more intimately. Lord, hear our cry. Let Your holy fire come down and bring revival to our hearts. Let it spread like fire in a dry field to all who now search in vain for meaning and hope in things that don't satisfy or last. Father, help us to be faithful in prayer and each day glorify You through our words and actions. Bind the Enemy and his schemes to deceive us, and to distort the purity you have called us to. Bind him in every way. And place a shield of protection around us. In Jesus' name, Amen.

CAN YOU IMAGINE
(Song)

Can you imagine a place of freedom
Where you walk the streets forgetting about yourself
Can you imagine a state of compassion
You see a broken person; you reach out your hand

I give it all 'cause my feet are getting tired
Nothing works when I try it on my own
Take it all 'cause my hands are hanging limp
Be my all, come use my life to shine
Be my all, refresh this heart of mine
Take it all so I don't have to just imagine

Can you imagine reflections of Jesus walking this earth
Overflowing with God's power and favor to serve
Can you imagine never feeling awkward
But living the fullest that He's called you to live each day

Can you imagine families mended
And giving bread to a hungry crying babe in Africa
Can you imagine rivers flowing in a dry land
And people praising God above for His power and love
Can you imagine nations singing in one chorus
Hallelujah, Hallelujah, Jesus saves.

Acknowledgments

I'm grateful to God for all He has done in my life. I'm an ordinary person, humbled by the great love God has for me and for each one of you.

Many people have blessed my life in many ways: my husband, David Bruce, whom I met after writing this book (a whole other story!), the man of my dreams, I love you. My father (whose eyes shine with God's love), for his unwavering support, enthusiasm, and discipline at the right time; my mother (an amazing warrior for God and an inspiration to many), for typing and editing my words, and for loving me and being my best friend; my brother, Steven, for his patience and words of wisdom when I needed them; John and Shary Vargo, for giving me wise counsel and being second parents to me; Bernie and Dar Koerselman, for their encouragement and prayers, and for spurring me on to write this book; Rose Simpson, for being my faithful friend; my Aunt Kathie, for advice on nutrition and being an inspiring example; my extended family—Shanna and all the Moes; Shannee my special cousin/sister; my cousins; my grandparents, Joan & George FitzGerald; Harold Moe "Poppop" (who is with the Lord) for being an example of a true warrior; the Butlers—Christina (Luv you! You have been an amazing friend!) and Shane, for their support; the Models for Christ team (both in New York and Atlanta); Lynne Rienstra, a mentor in speaking and writing, and an awesome prayer partner; my life-long friends from YWAM; our faithful supporters for enabling David and I to do mission work in the nations; Barbara from the Navigators; the Kregel crew—amazing people!—Paulette Zubel for editing and giving me a lot of encouragement; Scott Abbott for helping me edit!

The list could go on because many people have enriched my life. I thank each one of you.

I thank my Jesus for continuing to bring me through the refining fire, so that I may be as purified gold. Praise Him!

God bless you,
Natalie Moe
A Warrior for Christ

> *Now to him who is able to do immeasurably more than all we ask or imagine, according to his power that is at work within us, to him be glory in the church and in Christ Jesus throughout all generations, forever and ever! Amen.*
>
> Ephesians 3:20–21

IGNITE THE FIRE!

If you would like to receive information about
Natalie's other projects (including a CD from "Luminous,"
the band she performs with) please e-mail us at
ignitethefire@kregel.com.